1ˢᵗ Lt. Edward Turner Noland, Jr.
1917–1944

TEE
EDWARD TURNER NOLAN, JR.
BORN: 9-12-1917 ST. LOUIS, MO.
DIED: 11-18-1944 MODENA, ITALY

1st Lt. Edward Turner Noland, Jr.
1917–1944

SON, BROTHER, UNCLE, FRIEND, HERO

Genealogy House
Amherst, Massachusetts

Copyright 2016. All rights reserved.

Compiled by Kimberly Easter Noland

Published 2016 by
Genealogy House Publishers
Amherst, Massachusetts
Genealogyhouse.net

Cover and Book Design by
Douglas Lufkin
Lufkin Graphic Designs
www.LufkinGraphics.com

ISBN: 978-1-887043-33-5

Library of Congress Cataloging-in-Publication Data

Names: Noland, Kimberly Easter, 1974- compiler.
Title: 1st Lt. Edward Turner Noland, Jr. 1917/1944 : son, brother, uncle,
    friend, hero / compiled by Kimberly Easter Noland.
Other titles: First Lieutenant Edward Turner Noland, Jr. 1917/1944
Description: Amherst, Massachusetts : Genealogy House Publishers, [2016] |
    Includes bibliographical references.
Identifiers: LCCN 2016053029 | ISBN 9781887043335 (hardcover : alk. paper)
Subjects: LCSH: Noland, Edward Turner, Jr., 1917-1944. | United States. Army
    Air Forces. Bombardment Group (M), 310th--Biography. | Bombardiers--United
    States--Biography. | World War, 1939-1945--Aerial operations, American. |
    Nolan family. | Saint Louis (Mo.)--Biography.
Classification: LCC D790.253 310th .N65 2016 | DDC 940.54/4973092 [B] --dc23
LC record available at https://lccn.loc.gov/2016053029

Photographs, medals, and artifacts courtesy of the Noland family

This book is dedicated to all Noland family members who have preserved these archives, cherished the memories, and ensured Tee will never be forgotten. And to all future generations of Nolands: may we always honor the sacrifices this family, like thousands of American families, made for us.

Family of Edward Turner Noland and Florence Cole Miller Noland

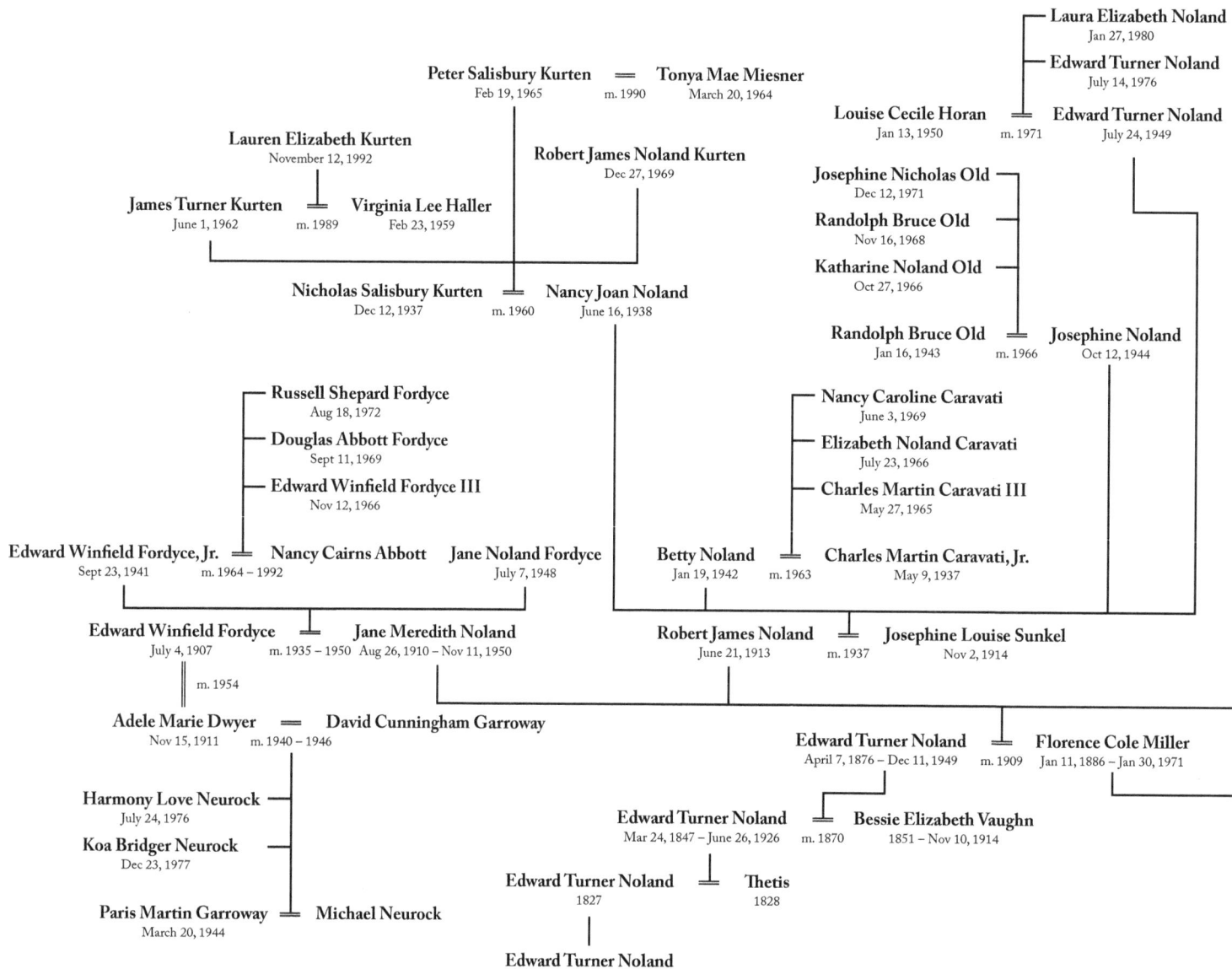

Laura Elizabeth Noland
Jan 27, 1980

Edward Turner Noland
July 14, 1976

Peter Salisbury Kurten = Tonya Mae Miesner
Feb 19, 1965   m. 1990   March 20, 1964

Louise Cecile Horan = Edward Turner Noland
Jan 13, 1950   m. 1971   July 24, 1949

Robert James Noland Kurten
Dec 27, 1969

Lauren Elizabeth Kurten
November 12, 1992

Josephine Nicholas Old
Dec 12, 1971

Randolph Bruce Old
Nov 16, 1968

Katharine Noland Old
Oct 27, 1966

James Turner Kurten = Virginia Lee Haller
June 1, 1962   m. 1989   Feb 23, 1959

Randolph Bruce Old = Josephine Noland
Jan 16, 1943   m. 1966   Oct 12, 1944

Nicholas Salisbury Kurten = Nancy Joan Noland
Dec 12, 1937   m. 1960   June 16, 1938

Russell Shepard Fordyce
Aug 18, 1972

Douglas Abbott Fordyce
Sept 11, 1969

Edward Winfield Fordyce III
Nov 12, 1966

Nancy Caroline Caravati
June 3, 1969

Elizabeth Noland Caravati
July 23, 1966

Charles Martin Caravati III
May 27, 1965

Edward Winfield Fordyce, Jr. = Nancy Cairns Abbott   Jane Noland Fordyce
Sept 23, 1941   m. 1964 – 1992   July 7, 1948

Betty Noland = Charles Martin Caravati, Jr.
Jan 19, 1942   m. 1963   May 9, 1937

Edward Winfield Fordyce = Jane Meredith Noland
July 4, 1907   m. 1935 – 1950   Aug 26, 1910 – Nov 11, 1950

Robert James Noland = Josephine Louise Sunkel
June 21, 1913   m. 1937   Nov 2, 1914

m. 1954

Adele Marie Dwyer = David Cunningham Garroway
Nov 15, 1911   m. 1940 – 1946

Edward Turner Noland = Florence Cole Miller
April 7, 1876 – Dec 11, 1949   m. 1909   Jan 11, 1886 – Jan 30, 1971

Harmony Love Neurock
July 24, 1976

Koa Bridger Neurock
Dec 23, 1977

Edward Turner Noland = Bessie Elizabeth Vaughn
Mar 24, 1847 – June 26, 1926   m. 1870   1851 – Nov 10, 1914

Paris Martin Garroway = Michael Neurock
March 20, 1944

Edward Turner Noland = Thetis
1827   1828

Edward Turner Noland

Original family tree, owned by Florence Cole Miller Noland, by Chas. O. Hoke, January 29, 1915.
Updated by Nancy Joan Noland Kurten, June 1992.

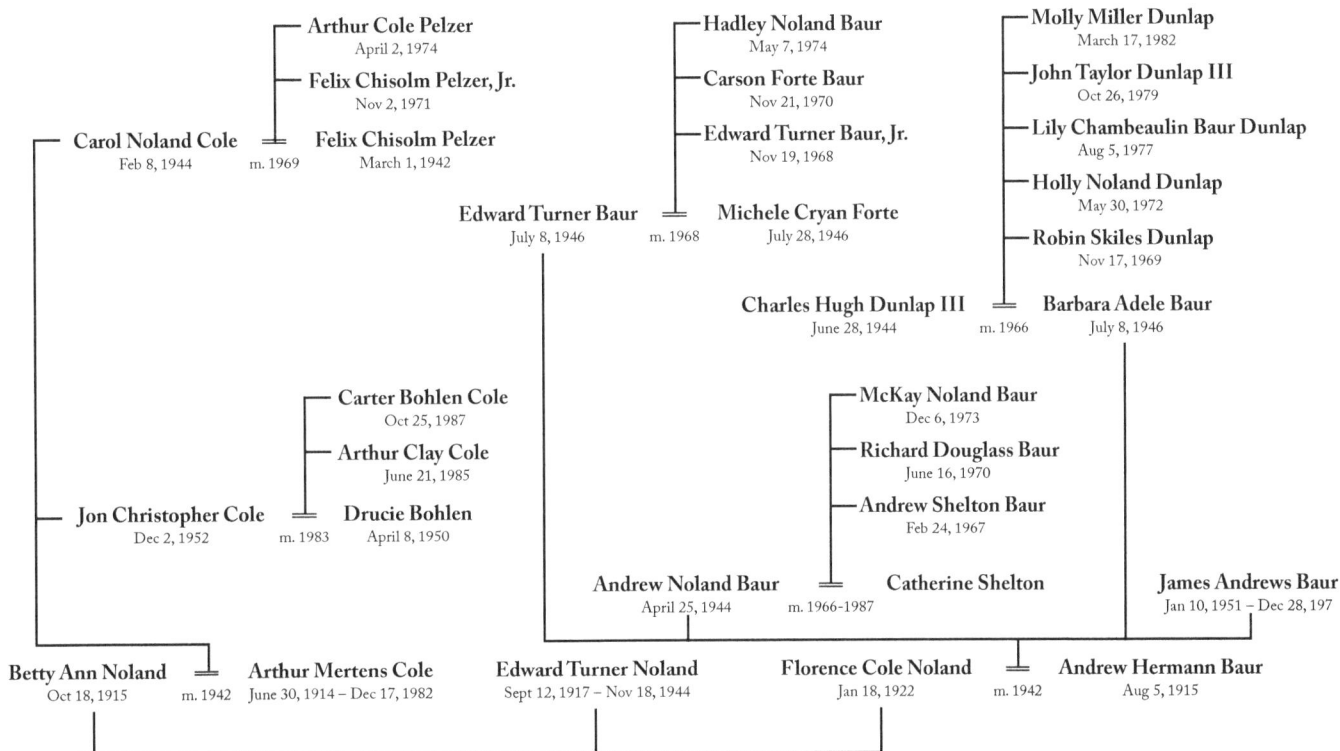

Arthur Cole Pelzer
April 2, 1974

Felix Chisolm Pelzer, Jr.
Nov 2, 1971

Carol Noland Cole ⚭ **Felix Chisolm Pelzer**
Feb 8, 1944   m. 1969   March 1, 1942

Hadley Noland Baur
May 7, 1974

Carson Forte Baur
Nov 21, 1970

Edward Turner Baur, Jr.
Nov 19, 1968

Edward Turner Baur ⚭ **Michele Cryan Forte**
July 8, 1946   m. 1968   July 28, 1946

Molly Miller Dunlap
March 17, 1982

John Taylor Dunlap III
Oct 26, 1979

Lily Chambeaulin Baur Dunlap
Aug 5, 1977

Holly Noland Dunlap
May 30, 1972

Robin Skiles Dunlap
Nov 17, 1969

Charles Hugh Dunlap III ⚭ **Barbara Adele Baur**
June 28, 1944   m. 1966   July 8, 1946

Carter Bohlen Cole
Oct 25, 1987

Arthur Clay Cole
June 21, 1985

Jon Christopher Cole ⚭ **Drucie Bohlen**
Dec 2, 1952   m. 1983   April 8, 1950

McKay Noland Baur
Dec 6, 1973

Richard Douglass Baur
June 16, 1970

Andrew Shelton Baur
Feb 24, 1967

Andrew Noland Baur ⚭ **Catherine Shelton**
April 25, 1944   m. 1966-1987

James Andrews Baur
Jan 10, 1951 – Dec 28, 197

Betty Ann Noland ⚭ **Arthur Mertens Cole**
Oct 18, 1915   m. 1942   June 30, 1914 – Dec 17, 1982

Edward Turner Noland
Sept 12, 1917 – Nov 18, 1944

Florence Cole Noland ⚭ **Andrew Hermann Baur**
Jan 18, 1922   m. 1942   Aug 5, 1915

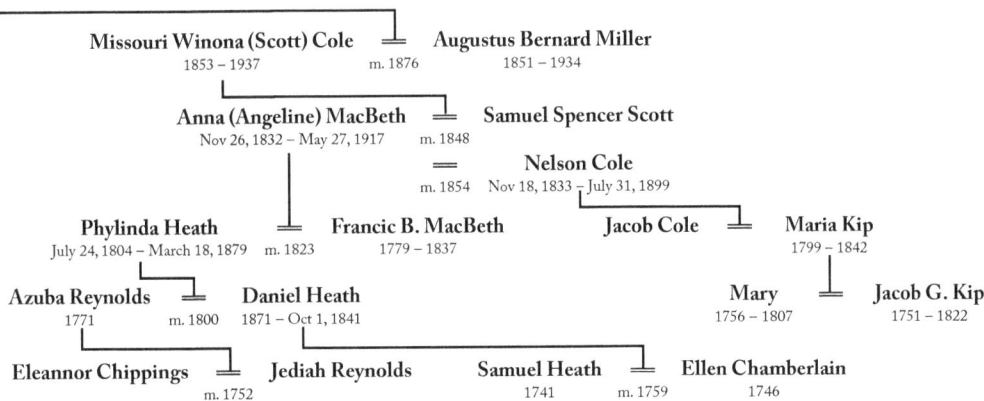

Missouri Winona (Scott) Cole ⚭ **Augustus Bernard Miller**
1853 – 1937   m. 1876   1851 – 1934

Anna (Angeline) MacBeth ⚭ **Samuel Spencer Scott**
Nov 26, 1832 – May 27, 1917   m. 1848

⚭ **Nelson Cole**
m. 1854   Nov 18, 1833 – July 31, 1899

Phylinda Heath ⚭ **Francie B. MacBeth**
July 24, 1804 – March 18, 1879   m. 1823   1779 – 1837

Jacob Cole ⚭ **Maria Kip**
1799 – 1842

Azuba Reynolds ⚭ **Daniel Heath**
1771   m. 1800   1871 – Oct 1, 1841

Mary   **Jacob G. Kip**
1756 – 1807   1751 – 1822

Eleannor Chippings ⚭ **Jediah Reynolds**
m. 1752

Samuel Heath ⚭ **Ellen Chamberlain**
1741   m. 1759   1746

— Contents —

— Prologue —

17 November 1944, Corsica, Italy

FIRST LIEUTENANT EDWARD[5] TURNER NOLAND, JR. was hanging around the Army base, waiting for a transport to take him back to the States. World War II was in full swing: "Tee," as he was known, was 27 years old. A bombardier, he had flown his quota of 25 missions in a B-25 bomber over North Africa, northern and southern Italy, southern France, and Yugoslavia and had earned the right to some well-deserved rest and recreation—R & R, the U.S. Army called it. He had also flown numerous reconnaissance missions; he no doubt was ready for a break. His fiancé, Patricia Sherertz perhaps hoped to see him; their engagement had been announced in the *Valley Morning Star*, Harlingen, Texas, on 9 July 1944.

But while he waited for the transport, Tee's good friend, Art Estley, the pilot with whom he had flown so many missions, tracked him down. Their plane, the "Miss Mitchell" had been grounded: a barrage of flak had hit them on a previous mission over southern France, and the plane was undergoing damage repairs. But Art told Tee he had flown an inventory plane the previous day, and the bombardier who'd flown with him had a medical issue. ("A cold" one newspaper reported; "a nervous breakdown," the family was later told.) Whatever the reason, Art was without a bombardier; he had a mission scheduled for the next day.

"I know you're heading back," Art said, "but we're supposed to hit a rail yard tomorrow in Modena. We're the lead plane. And I need you."

The lead plane in a squadron of bombers was of critical importance. The rail yard was important, too; it was a central point in Italy through which the Germans brought guns and ammunition. And Tee was the kind of guy who never wanted to let down a friend.

— Chapter 1 —

Edward[5] Turner "Tee" Noland was born 12 September 1917 in St. Louis, Missouri. He was the fourth child (later there would be five) and second son of Edward[4] Turner Noland (b. 7 April 1876; d. 11 Dec 1949) and Florence Cole Miller (b. 11 Jan 1886; d. 30 Jan 1971).

He was not the first Edward Turner Noland. Earlier generations of the family had arrived in the United States from Belfast, Ireland through England. They first settled in Virginia, but by the mid-1800s they were living in Missouri; the 1840 Census reports that Tee's great-great-grandfather Edward[1] Turner Noland, was involved in agriculture in Jackson County. He had a wife and five children, including a son, Edward[2] Turner Noland (b. in 1827).

At some point, Edward[2] moved to Hickman Mills, a small town south of Kansas City, where he became a lumber merchant and married a woman named Thetis (b. in 1828). The couple had three children; one of their sons was named Edward[3] Turner Noland (b. 24 March 1847; d. 26 June 1926). In 1862, Edward[2] joined the Confederate forces in the Civil War (also known as the War Between the States). As the quartermaster of his battalion, he was in charge of supplies. Copies of his requisitions for mules have been kept in the family records.

When Edward[3] grew up, he worked for the *Kansas City Times*, an area newspaper. He also was a gentleman farmer, with a love for pigs and cows, hens, and horses. He married Bessie Elizabeth Vaughn (b. in 1851; d. 14 Nov 1914), who had been born in Kentucky and had a twin sister, Bell. The girls' mother had died in childbirth; their father was so distraught, he went away to "seek fame and fortune." Before returning, however, he contracted yellow fever and died. The twin babies were taken to Independence, Missouri to live with an aunt.

Edward[3] and Bessie had seven children: Vaughn, Bessie B., **Edward[4]**, Harry, twins Mary (tall and thin) and Margaret (short and round), and Garland. In 1886, the family made plans to move to Cape Girardeau, Missouri. Edward[4] had, by then, completed the fourth grade; it was decided he would go to St. Louis to live with family friends, the McCoys. (Legend has it that they were related to the McCoys of the feuding Hatfields and McCoys!)

In Cape Girardeau, Edward[3] was engaged in farming and merchandising. He also served as sheriff, collector of Cape Girardeau, and later, as Missouri State Treasurer for a year. In 1894, the family moved to St. Louis, and Edward[3] was in the insurance business; in 1910, Census records reported that he was a hotelkeeper in Farmington, Missouri.

In the meantime, Edward[4] was growing up. His first job was delivering telegrams. The tobacco industry was booming in the twentieth century, and Edward[4] went on to work at Drummond Tobacco Company, on Park Avenue near Vandeventer in St. Louis. He started in the factory where large tobacco leaves were first dried, then ground into finer leaves for cigarettes, cigars, and chewing tobacco.

At some point, Edward[4] met Florence Miller, the daughter of Missouri Scott Cole and Augustus "Gus" Bernard Miller.

Missouri Scott Cole was the daughter of Samuel Spencer Scott and Anna MacBeth Scott. Unfortunately, Samuel died shortly after Missouri and her brother, Charles, were born. Anna then married Nelson Cole, who legally adopted Missouri and Charles. The couple went on to have five biological children together. Anna was of Scottish descent and Presbyterian; she was born in Indiana, and was the daughter of Phylinda Heath and Francis B. MacBeth. Nelson, a major in the Union forces, became a successful lumber businessman. His family had a farm in Lebanon, Illinois, where Nelson helped found McKendree College.

Florence's mother, Missouri, was kind and gentle. She walked with a limp, which was a result of polio. As an adult, she was only five feet tall. Florence's father, Gus, had roots that went back to Germany. His father had come to the United States from Stuttgart as a brewmaster for Anheuser Busch. One family story implies that Gus's original family name was spelled Muller, the German version of Miller. And though Florence's birth certificate states her name as Muller, and that she was born in 1886 on Gratiot Street in St. Louis, the census records always listed the family name as Miller. In those days, people were not fond of the Germans; apparently Gus had decided to hide the true spelling of his name.

Gus and Missouri were married at the Cole's residence on 815 Taylor Ave. in St. Louis on 15 June 1876. The couple had eight children, though only five survived. Florence was the middle child; her older siblings were Anna and Charles; her younger siblings were Bernard and Meredith.

Florence grew up in the house at 815 Taylor Ave. and at 1615 Grand Avenue. (Note: Her brother Bernard, or "Bud," achieved fame when he ranked fourth in his class at West Point. He served during World War I, attaining the rank of major. He served as chief engineer, Corps of Engineers, with the American Forces in Germany. He died from influenza in 1921.)

Florence married Edward[4] in St. Peter's Episcopal Church in St. Louis on 30 October 1909. Their first home was an apartment at 4943 Laclede Ave., between Euclid and Kings Highway. In 1910, their first child, Jane Meredith, named after Florence's brother, was born. In 1913, a son Robert James (called "Bob") came along. He was named after two of Edward[4]'s bosses, Robert D. Lewis and James A.W. Lewis. Bob was quite sick as a child and was, at one point, purportedly carried around on a pillow. However, the boy grew up to be "full of nonsense," according to his youngest sibling.

A girl named Betty Ann followed Bob in 1915, then came **Edward**[5] in 1917. Officially recorded as Edward, Jr., he was called "Tee" by the family. The couple's final child, Florence Cole, was born in 1922.

While the children were growing up, Edward[4] continued his work in the tobacco industry. He was a bookkeeper and later in charge of production for Drummond, which, along with Liggett & Myers Tobacco Company, was part of American Tobacco Company. Edward[4] stayed with Drummond until American Tobacco broke up, then Drummond became Liggett & Myers. The primary product manufactured at the St. Louis plant was chewing tobacco. (With an increasing popularity of cigarettes, in 1915 the company's flagship brand became *Chesterfield*; in 1926 they became the first tobacco company to market their product to women.[1])

Edward[4] Turner Noland at work.

Edward[4] was known at work for always wearing a hat: an outside hat and an inside hat. When he'd arrive at the office, he'd replace his outside hat with his inside hat, which he'd wear all day while inspecting the factory. At one point he apparently had been asked to become president of Liggett & Myers, but the position would have meant moving with Florence and their five children to New York City. Florence said, "No!" Edward[4] was subsequently appointed secretary-treasurer, a post at which he remained until his retirement in 1944. In addition to his work at the company, he served on the Board of Directors of the Mercantile Bank in St. Louis. At the time of his death in 1949, the bank had a hand-lettered memorial book created to honor his extensive service.

Tee and Florence.

This generation's first family home was on Woodlawn Ave. in Kirkwood, about fourteen miles southwest of St. Louis. The house was near the railroad tracks and across the street from an Episcopal church, which, according to family legend, burned on the night Bob was born (21 June 1913). Documentation of that incident, however, is not available.

Much of the children's early childhood was spent in a two-story, brick house at 6011 Enright Ave., St. Louis. One block east from what became the new Delmar train station in 1928 (also called the Wabash Railroad Delmar Station), the area appears to have been a busy family neighborhood with treed green lawns in what's now referred to as an "urban village."

The family seemed to enjoy animals. Bob built a shed in the backyard on Enright Ave. and kept his pony named Billy there. Stray dogs also seemed to "find" Bob, and he sometimes brought them home.

With the children then quite young, their maternal grandparents, Missouri and Gus Miller, spent a lot of time there. According to Jeannette Lichtenstein—a former neighbor who'd lived at 5967 Enright Ave.—the children referred to their maternal grandmother, Missouri, as "Nana," and they called their maternal grandfather, Gus, "One-Two." Apparently while teaching Jane to count, Gus often called out: "One-two, one-two!" One day, Jane saw him getting out of the car, and she said, "One-two!" to everyone's delight. Jeannette also remembered that Gus wore shiny shoes and that on Sundays he always arrived with candy Lifesavers and small molasses candies called Yellow Jackets for the children tucked in his pocket.

In 1925, the family moved to 21 Washington Terrace, a lovely, spacious, three-story stone home that they soon referred to as "Club 21." They did not have electric lights; each evening a

The Noland house at 21 Washington Terrace, St. Louis, Missouri.

lamplighter would walk down the street carrying his ladder, stopping along the way to ignite each gas streetlamp. At one point they had a radio in the sunroom that provided much entertainment, as did roller-skating, sports—especially baseball in summer months—, and playing lots of games, including card games that Edward[4] enjoyed. He also liked to get down on all fours and shoot marbles with Tee and Florence.

Sundays were family days in the Noland household. They all stayed home (not even a trip to the movies was allowed), although visitors were always welcome.

Edward[4] had a wonderful sense of humor. He was a kind and responsible man who was highly respected in the community. Behind the scenes, he took care of his two maiden sisters for much of their lives. (After Gus died in 1934, Nana moved from their apartment on Lafayette Ave., west of Grand, into the Washington Terrace home.)

In addition to being a successful businessman, Edward[4] loved being outdoors. He was a beautiful figure skater, logged three holes-in-one playing golf, and, according to his daughter Florence, "You didn't want to be on the other side of a tennis court from him."

Some of the children began their educations at Hamilton Elementary School. The new, 24-room brick schoolhouse opened in 1918 and had an enrollment of more than 1,000 students. Jane graduated from Hosmer Hall, a private girls' school that had been founded in 1884, but closed in 1936. Bob and Tee completed high school at St. Louis Country Day School, which was out in Ferguson near what later became the airport; Betty and Florence graduated from Country Day School's sister school for girls, Mary Institute. It is interesting to note that the founder of Washington University, William Greenleaf Eliot, established

Four of the Noland children: Top row from left, Betty and Robert; bottom row from left, Florence and Tee.

Mary Institute and the predecessor to Country Day School, Smith Academy (1854), to prepare students for the university. One notable student at Smith Academy (and a kindergartner at Mary Institute) was Eliot's grandson T.S. Eliot, who, in 1948, won the Nobel Prize in Literature.

As his father before him, Edward[4] also loved farming. Around the same time he bought the Washington Terrace house, he also purchased thirty-two acres of land on Conway and Mason Roads, for which he paid three dollars an acre—reportedly the highest price to date paid for acreage in St. Louis County. Originally called "The Potato Patch" because the previous owners had farmed potatoes on the land, Edward[4] renamed it "Broadview," because from the front of the hill at night he could see the headlights of cars several miles away on Olive Street Road.

He soon had a barn built at Broadview that housed some cows and a tractor. Later, that first barn became a summer home and a larger barn was built for his growing herd of farm animals: cows, horses, and sheep. Out in the woods, a chicken house and a turkey house were added. He even owned goats until one got onto the roof of their Cadillac Touring Car and ate the canvas top. Edward[4] also developed an interest in gardening and tree grafting, and was so proud of a one-pound peach that appeared on one tree, he had it carefully wrapped, packed into a tobacco crate, and shipped to his bosses at Liggett & Myers in New York City.

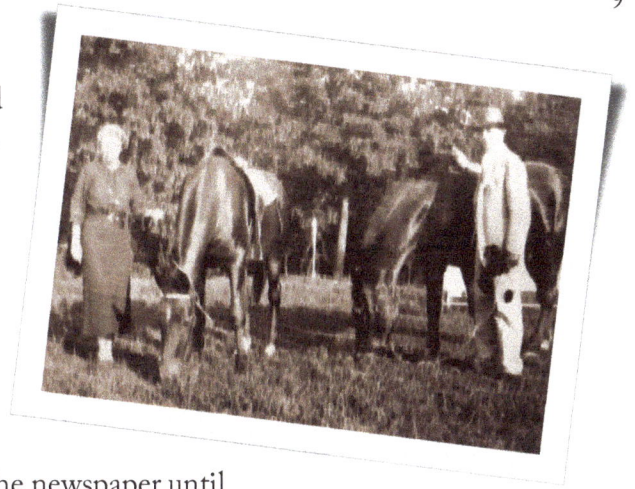

Edward[4] with his wife, Florence, at Broadview.

With a growing family, the days and nights were structured and orderly. The children were not allowed to use the front door, only the back; and they were not allowed to look at the newspaper until their father had finished with it.

On weekday evenings, Edward[4] arrived home at 6:00p.m.; at 6:15 the family was seated together in the dining room of the Washington Terrace home. Betty sat next to her mother on one side of the table and often wrapped food she didn't like into a napkin for later, secret disposal; Florence sat on the other side, when she sat. Most of the time Florence was in the kitchen nibbling on chocolate cake that the cook regularly provided.

Once, when Edward[4] was asked the cost of his milk bill for his five growing children, he replied, "About two hundred dollars a week!" He then explained that he bought the cows, grew the feed, and paid the farmhands to take care of the cows and milk them—all of which, on average, totaled two hundred dollars a week.

Life was active for Tee and his brothers and sisters. Their next-door neighbors, the Fordyces (cousins of Edward Fordyce who later married the eldest Noland, Jane) included boys, who loved to play pranks with a live alligator they kept in their attic. One evening, with the help of the Noland boys, they let it down the stairs into the middle of a large, formal party.

Every two years, Edward[4] purchased new cars—a four-door model for himself; a large touring car with jump seats for Florence. Both vehicles typically had big running boards and often were Pierce Arrows (and an occasional Cadillac), bought from Mr. Papin, an area car dealer. Invariably, Mr. Papin would arrive with a new car to test drive just as the family sat down to dinner. Everything stopped and they all bundled into the car and took a drive through Forest Park.

Most important to note about the cars were the famous Noland license plates that all began with the number "21," to honor the home at 21 Washington Terrace. At some point, Edward[4] had a "woody" station wagon that bore the plate number 2124. (Numbers 2125 and 2127 remain in the family as of this writing.)

The front living room, or parlor, at the Washington Terrace house was called the Music Room. Jane often played "Indian Love Call" on the huge grand piano; Tee—who did not read music—played the piano, guitar, and almost any instrument he picked up.

"Family" was important to Edward[4] and Florence. They often held family reunions in Farmington, Missouri, with Edward[4]'s parents, brothers Harry and Garland, and sisters, Aunt Bell and Mary Chinn, Margaret Crawford, and their families. The Farmington twang was not to be forgotten!

While the children were growing up, weekends were spent at Broadview. When Bob was older and dating Jo Sunkel, the couple, along with Tee and Florence, rolled the clay tennis court. Tennis "tournaments" evolved, with prizes provided by Edward[4]'s friend, Abe Abrams.

Fascinated by real estate, Edward[4] added "Longview" at Clayton and Mason Farms to his portfolio—seventy acres of rolling fields for crops and livestock, and woods that bordered Mason Road. He modernized the house on the property that had been built around an original log cabin, and in the late 1930s, when Florence suffered a heart attack, he had a bedroom configured on the first floor.

Front Row: Florence Noland Baur [5]; Gran – Florence Miller Noland; Granddad – Edward Turner Noland; Child: Carol Noland Cole, daughter of Betty and Art, approximately age 4; Jane Noland Fordyce [1] (oldest child).
Back Row: Robert James Noland [2]; Andrew Hermann Baur; Betty Noland Cole [3]; Arthur Mertens Cole.

As time passed, the children grew up and began to marry. Jane married Edward Fordyce in 1935; Bob wed Jo in 1937; Florence married Andrew Baur in the summer of 1942—unlike other boys Florence had dated, Tee had "approved" of him as a brother-in-law. Florence and Andy's wedding reception was held at Longview with the wedding table set up on the porch, and tables for guests on the lawn. Among the guests were Art Cole, a young man from Ohio who was working in St. Louis for Dupont and was dating Betty (they married on the day after Christmas that year), and Jane Rickey, a friend of Tee's. Most special for Florence was that Tee had been able to get a military leave to be there, too.

Then the family began to expand with grandchildren, too: Nancy Noland in 1938, Edward Fordyce (called Windy) in 1941, then Nancy's sister, Betty, in 1942. Edward[4] and Florence had become Gran and Grandad.

Over the years, many additions were made to the Longview house: barns were built; gardens were planted. A huge turkey called "Tom" ran the barnyard. There were horses for Gran, cows, chickens, pigs, and sheep. Grandad had hunting dogs, a German shepherd named Bum, a collie named Puck, and Tee's little dog, named Sporty. The fields were filled with alfalfa, wheat, and corn; the garden held asparagus, tomatoes, simlins (yellow squash), okra, and raspberries. There was a grape arbor, a large flower garden with a birdbath, and a special birdhouse for purple martins.

At Broadview, Grandad bred Belgium Percheron horses and raised jersey cows from the Isle of Jersey: He was very proud of a set of twin calves born one spring.

In 1944, Carol Cole, Drew Baur, and Jody Noland were all born; the Noland family was bustling with activity and joy. Until everything abruptly—and forever—changed.

— Chapter 2 —

7 December 1943

Dear Florence,

. . . Mother had written to me about Aunt Bess being very
ill . . . If there is anything I can do let me know right away.
I wish it was possible for me to be there, because I feel that
having us around, or knowing we were there, would help her
to get well quicker . . .

Love to all,

Tee

[See Appendix A for reproduction of letter.]

As WITH THE REST OF THE NOLANDS, family was clearly important to Tee. Yet, from early on, he was a prankster, a bit of a rebel, and an enigma to his father, who once had commented that he couldn't quite figure Tee out.

Well-liked by his classmates, Tee was always adventuresome, and not above playing a joke or two. For example, he used to take the streetcar to St Louis Country Day School; one day, along with a couple of his friends, he figured out a way to derail the streetcar so they couldn't make it to school.

Incredibly artistic and a gifted musician, Tee played ukulele, guitar, piano, trumpet, and trombone. The fact that he couldn't read music never held him back; it was reported that he was always a big hit at parties . . . especially when he played piano and danced simultaneously. He also played football, basketball, and baseball, and when friends needed advice, they turned to him. Some said he was a natural-born leader.

Tee loved going to Broadview Farm, where a favorite summer pastime was to go out to one of the two big ponds on the property with his siblings Bob and Florence and shoot snakes and turtles with 22-pistols. In fact, Tee would sit patiently by the water's edge for hours at a time, waiting for a snake's head to pop up, then he would, as Florence related, "pick him off." In winter, the ponds froze over and they all ice skated.

And though they loved spending summers on the farm, the children also were treated to family vacations in Michigan, on Nantucket, and they even once traveled to California by train.

Tee and Florence at the historic Edgewater Beach Hotel, Chicago, Illinois

In high school, Florence—who idolized her older brother—introduced Tee to a girl named Sue Rickey. Sue was the daughter of Branch Rickey, the owner of the St. Louis Browns baseball team and later member of the Baseball Hall of Fame.

It wasn't long before Sue became Tee's girlfriend; they loved riding horses together at the farm. And though they had been raised with household help, their mother had instilled in the children that they should never ask anyone to do something that they hadn't done, so Tee and Florence made it a point to curry their own horses.

Tee was quite handsome, with a happy smile and a mischievous twinkle in his eyes. He grew to be 6'2", which was very tall for a young man in the 1930s; his friends often called him Big Ed. In 2012, his great-nephew, Carson Baur, reported on Fold3.com[2] that Tee was "quite debonair and popular with the ladies. Not as much of a scholar but certainly a jolly good fellow . . . much to his father's dismay." Tee apparently also had a bad habit of never being able to keep a gas tank filled. On weekends, he often begged his brother, Bob, to let him borrow his car. Then, on Monday mornings, when it was time to go to work, Bob wandered around town, trying to find his car, knowing that Tee would have left it wherever it had run out of gas.

Edward[1] and his wife, Florence, at the beach.

After high school graduation, Tee enrolled in college — first at Washington University in St. Louis. He then went on to the University of North Carolina . . . although instead

Tee, perhaps in the Ford V8 as be called it in his poem on page 19.

of attending classes, he could often be found on Delmar Boulevard practicing with a group of jazz musicians. He played the guitar, piano, and, according to his niece, Nancy, he played "almost every other instrument by ear."

By this time, his niece Nancy had grown close to her Uncle Tee. She always thought he was a "really cool guy." He was fun and silly; she remembered that a room upstairs at Longview was called "Tee's Room." It was pine-paneled and, she thinks, had red curtains. He called her "Little Barnsmell" and called himself "Big Barnsmell," which Nancy decided were pretty fancy nicknames.

She also has treasured the following poem that Tee wrote in honor of the barn that was renovated into a house that the family later called "home" on Broadview Farm:

> *EPIC OF BROADVIEW*
> *Foist it was a garage*
> *Wit grease spots around*
> *And dat ornery brown and white thing,*
> *Pat, the lousy hound.*
>
> *There was folding doors in front*
> *And a cold concrete floor*
> *And the foist dat a feller heard*
> *Vas de Old Man's snore.*
>
> *Den we put in vooden block*
> *And stained them mahogany brown*
> *And Celotex was plastered*
> *On de walls and all around.*
>
> *Da next year brought de dormers*
> *Wit de sleeping porch for Puger*
> *And a dining room on de foist floor,*
> *Big Shot, pass de sugar.*

Den ve put in running water
And a tub for Ma and Pa to bathe
But de water vas too cold yet
So all de Old Man did vas to wade.

Ve got a john yet, too
And everybody's happy.
Of all de rooms within the house
De Blue Room vas most snappy.

And de old place don't look the same
Wit knotty pine and, let me see,
I guess now we'll give a parking space
To Smitty and to Tee.

And now among the old apple trees
Nestles a foist class home,
Ve done got rid of de old gray mare
And put Revely und Grupp on de roam.

And Puger has a stable
Wit Chessie, Lady and Grainger.
And Tee in his Ford V8
Has become a highway ranger.

But wait what's that
A raisin' all the fuss ?
Oh, never mind, it's only Betty
In Ma's old black hearse!

ETN, Jr.   "Uncle Tee"
4.13.1938

He also took flying lessons and dreamed of becoming a pilot. His wish would come true in a much different way than he might have imagined: In August 1941, with World War II underway in Europe, Tee was one of the first draftees during peacetime in the United States.

Tee in Brooks Field, July 1943

Tee's first stop was at Officer Candidate School in Fort Leavenworth, Kansas, where he was commissioned as a second lieutenant in the Calvary. But because Tee really wanted to fly, he was transferred to the Air Corps at Brooks Field in Texas and began training to become a co-pilot. He received his wings after completing navigation and radio courses; then he decided to become a bombardier.

("One thing was never enough for him," his sister Florence later recalled with a laugh. "Tee always had to do more.")

He was then transferred to Harlington, Texas, where he soon graduated from the gunnery school.

Crouched under the Plexiglas dome in the nose of the B-25 Mitchell Bomber, Tee apparently found a comfortable home. Called the Norden Bomb Site, the small space contained 13, .50-caliber machine guns and some 5,000[3] pounds of bombs, which could not be activated to be dropped until the plane was over its target. That way, if the mission was scrubbed or other issues arose, the plane would not have to land with its bombs already activated. . . a situation that would likely blow the plane up. Each plane consisted of a crew that included:

- pilot
- co-pilot
- bombardier
- radio operator
- gunner
- tail gunner

Tee's first assignment was as a bombardier instructor. While still in Harlington, he frequently played his guitar and a ukulele in his barracks.

And he met a young woman named Patricia Sheretz, who he later described in the 7 December 1943 letter to Florence as "a swell girl" *[see Appendix A]*.

He had yet to see any action, but in a letter to Edward[4], Florence, and Andy *[see Appendix B]* on 31 January 1944, Tee wrote:

> *I will write again before I leave and give you the final low down. Be good and when I get back we will have some fun, after I get married, which will be the first day I am back. I'm tired of living among men and by myself.*

Before leaving, Tee also made sure that his little dog, Sporty, would be cared for by his brother Bob and family in his absence.

Then on the envelope of a 4 March letter to Tee's parents, the return address was A.P.O. New York City, indicating that Tee had been sent overseas as a member of a squadron—121st Liaison Squadron—of B-25s to North Africa. The previous year, the Axis forces, under the leadership of Nazi Brigadier General Erwin Rommel (also known as "The Desert Fox") had lost the battle to gain control of the Suez Canal. The defeat prevented the Germans from gaining critical access to oil in the Middle East and to other raw materials from Asia, yet the Allies apparently still wanted to ramp up their air power. Situated not far from Italy, the North Africa location offered strategic proximity for the European campaigns.[4]

In addition to his regular duties in the B-25s, Tee flew "Mosquito" reconnaissance planes, crossing German lines at night, surveying the landscape in order to assess damage after air strikes.

In that 4 March letter, he revealed *[see Appendix C]* that he had told the family about his marriage plans to Pat the previous December, at which time it was expected that the wedding would take place at the end of May. He wrote:

> *It seemed far away in December when I told you of my plans, but it seems much father away now, except that I feel everything is set and OK. Just a matter of time . . .*

He continued the letter on a playful note:

> *You will find her relatively inexperienced and actually a young girl, but anything I want is what she wants, and I guess from her letters to me she feels the sun rises and sets on me . . . She said she hoped we would have five sons and a daughter or two, but boys are her main wish . . . I am nine years older than she is, but she knows what she wants and has wonderful taste in clothes and everything (including men! Ahem!).*

In another letter to Florence on 27 March 1944 *[see Appendix D]*, Tee dated it at the top and added "Somewhere in North Africa." He was most concerned about his sister's impending baby, and made it a point to write:

> *When you go into the hospital, remember you have a brother someplace over here that won't be too busy to think of you then, and I shall worry about it until I hear that everything is all right.*

It was also evident that he knew he would not be staying in North Africa:

> *I believe I will have my own plane when I finally reach my destination. It will be a relief.*

At some point (it is unclear whether Tee was granted a leave while in North Africa), he either brought home or sent a small wooden box to his mother. His niece Nancy remembered it clearly.

In any event, by 7 May 1944, his squadron had changed: The return address on a letter to his sister Jane *[see Appendix E]* reads: 3rd Bomb. Trng. Sq. However, he was apparently still in North Africa.

In that letter (only a portion of it remains), it is evident again that staying engaged with the family seemed important to Tee. He expressed hope that Jane's husband, Ed, had obtained a commission in the navy. "He will be much better off than in the army," Tee wrote. "I wouldn't trade, but I am a little younger than Ed and I am a little more used to not counting definitely on anything."

Though we can't be sure what he meant by that last line, Tee continued to show his concern for the family and the on-going closeness he felt to them all. After commenting on Jane's son Windy contracting the measles, he said:

> *Jane, I sure hope you move out with the family if Ed goes into the army or navy. It would mean an awful lot to Dad & Mom. I have never told them, but one of the things that has always hurt me whenever I came home on a leave is how lonesome they both are. It hurt just sitting at the dinner table with them and realizing they are finally alone. Of course I knew it must be, but mark my word, they will have a happier life with you and Florence with them. I intend to spend all of my leave with them when I get back, except about five days when I am married.*

A week later, on 14 May, he wrote again, that time to his sister Florence after learning of the birth of Florence and Andy's son, Drew. The letter *[see Appendix F]*, in part, reads:

*Congratulations! I knew it would be a boy but I didn't want
to get your hopes up. I sure am glad you didn't have too much
trouble or pain. I know Andy must be very happy . . . I can
see you and Betty fighting over the tub to see who gets to wash
diapers first.*

(Tee's older sister, Betty, had given birth to a daughter, Carol Cole,
two and a half months earlier.)

Later in that same letter he gave a rare account of what he was actually
doing in North Africa:

*. . . My duties are entirely disassociated with my old ones. I
am in an entirely different outfit. I would tell you all about it
except that everyone would think up a hundred new worries.
I will tell you this much: I am not in four-motored bombers
so Mother ought to be glad because she said she didn't like
them. I am in a bombardment squadron and have been flying
around three hours a day. For your added info, they don't
have commissioned gunners except for teaching, so I'm not
a gunner. Now all you have to do is think of my training in
Texas, look at the type of outfit I am in, and you can see what
I'm doing. That's Right! Bombing!*

Then he added:

*. . . I hope I will get my missions in quick and the war will be
over because I am awfully anxious to get back. As for what I
am going to do when the war is over, I don't know, and it will
mean that I will be married long before then, but I just plain
don't care to blow any bubbles about that this far ahead . . .*

I love all of you very much (of course Pat is a little different kind of love). Don't worry about me because everything is and will be fine. We had a hell of a sandstorm last night, but today was perfect . . .

Two weeks later, another letter arrived, again from North Africa. The thin tissue of the "Air Mail" stationary was dotted with what appeared to be burn spots from cigarette ash. Perhaps he was smoking while writing the letter; perhaps he was in deep thought for the words he was about to write to his "baby" sister *[see Appendix G]*:

May 31st, 1944
North Africa

My Dear Florence —

I am very happy to hear that Junior is doing so well, and that you are getting along fine. Your last V mail has started me wondering a little bit about something, so I'll have to tell you just in case I am right, there will be someone who understands—so—

Some time ago, before Easter, I wrote Bob [their elder brother] and Jo [Bob's wife] a note in which I told them that in the event I should not get back to the States, and if the family was informed I was missing in action, then (and then only) I wanted them to name their first boy after Dad for me . . . This is strictly between you and me. I don't mind if you tell Andy, but under no circumstances . . . are Mother and Dad to know . . . I would rather not have Mother worrying about me not getting back. I can't stop Pat from worrying, but Mother has enough others & not as much spare time as Pat.

He closed the letter with: "Be good, squirt," a favorite nickname he had for Florence.

Whatever had triggered his wary thoughts, Tee went back to work and carried on. And his squadron moved on to Corsica.

be harmful if we are shot down

BOOK No. 1.

— Chapter 3 —

T EE WAS OFFICIALLY ASSIGNED to the 380th Bombardment Squadron, 310th Bombardment Group in the Mediterranean Theater. While on bombing missions, in order to hit their targets, the planes flew at 3,000 feet—an altitude at which the plane was not pressurized. Unfortunately, at that low altitude, they were clearly visible to the Germans.

Tee's log that he marked "Book No. 1" tells so much: The entries are comprehensive, fascinating, and, most of all, chilling. The text follows along with editorial comments in [brackets] and simultaneous events noted as appropriate. *[See Appendix H for a complete reproduction of the actual log in Tee's handwriting.]*

RECORD—
T. Noland Jr.
Bombardment Squadron,
Bombardment Group.

The following experiences
in the War with Germany
are my own, and I start
this record in Ghissonachia,
Corsica, July 2nd, 1944
after serving two years
and eleven months in the
U.S. Army Air Forces.

All accounts of ensuing
missions are written after
the Bombing as no personal
possessions go with us lest it
be harmful if we are shot down

Sunday, July 2nd, 8:00A.M.

This is my first bomb mission, and I fully realize I know nothing of war. The feeling before takeoff is very similar to the tension before a football game.

At 8:00a.m. we climbed in our B-25 and started the engines. At eight-twenty we, with the rest of our sqdn. [squadron] are airborne. The target is a vital viaduct NE of Florence, Italy, which the Germans are using as a supply route. We crossed the blue water of Gurian Sea and into Allied-held Italy 3 miles N. of Talamong. We proceeded (after one crew member hollered, "Ladies and gents, this is Italy!") to Foligno where we turned north into German held territory. It looked the same as any other to me on this Sunday until 5 minutes later when I saw a black burst of the filthiest color imaginable. This was the first flak I have ever seen.

During the next twenty minutes we dodged and wove in and out of those bursts, and I hurriedly put on my flak vest and helmet, at the same time looking at our other ships with black bursting all around us. We ran through the puffs, and [the] explosions of the 88mm. shells shook the Mitchells like dead leaves. So far everything was fine.

We arrived at Appechio for our next change of course and headed for Dicomanu to the north. The flak grew more intense and the tail gunner shouted, "For Christ's sake get out of here!" I felt the same. You simply sit and wait for the fragments to hit.

We had not long to wait for in the next two minutes we were hit by five pieces but not damaged outside of holes. The rest of our formation took it too, and as I sat there with all the glass around me I prayed to come out all right. We had been told there would be FW190s & ME109s, but none got close as our Spitfire cover kept them away.

We finally flew over our initial point to begin our bomb run on Borgo, San Lorenzo. Three minutes later I watched the bombay [bomb bay] doors swing open on the lead ship and all of the others. Twenty seconds later we released our 4,000 lbs. (per ship) of bombs and banked away. I have never before seen such an explosion & columns of smoke and dust.

We were halfway through and on our way home through the same gauntlet of ack ack. There were deafening roars when the big shells burst around us. Shortly afterward I felt a pain in my left shoulder and looked at the plexiglas overhead. There were two holes and two more about two inches wide through the floor. The shattering glass had hit me on the shoulder (no damage) and the flak passed about 3 inches from me on its way through. We called the

A German Focke-Wulf FW 190

Messerschmitt BF 109

*gunners and radio operator and found them
all ok and I thanked God for his help.*

*We flew for about fifteen minutes more to
our part of Italy & home the same route.*

*When we landed we counted 15 flak holes
in our ship, and I said to myself, "I've had it!"
I felt like a member of the team now. My first
successful mission.*

Back home in the United States, 2 July 1944 was another special day in Tee's life: it was the day his engagement to Pat Sheretz was officially announced at a tea that the *St. Louis Dispatch* later reported was held "at the home of Miss Sheretz's brother-in-law and sister, Lt. Col. And Mrs. Virgil L. Zoller, with whom she and her mother live." [Tee's sister Betty was also there.] The article went on to say: "The wedding will take place soon after Lt. Noland's return to the United States." It was noted that the bride-to-be was expected to be "in St. Louis the last of August to visit her fiancé's parents, Mr. and Mrs. Edward Turner Noland, at their country place on Clayton Road."

Later the *St. Louis Dispatch* reported: "On the day his engagement was announced, July 2, 2nd Lt. Edward T. Noland Jr. celebrated by blasting the viaduct west of Borgo San Lorence in Italy."

It apparently wasn't long before Tee became good friends with his pilot, First Lieutenant Art Ensley. At some point the crew had named their B-25 the "Miss Mitchell." (The manufacturer, North American Aviation, called the plane the B-25 Mitchell, in honor of Major General William "Billy" Mitchell, who had been "a pioneer of U.S. Military

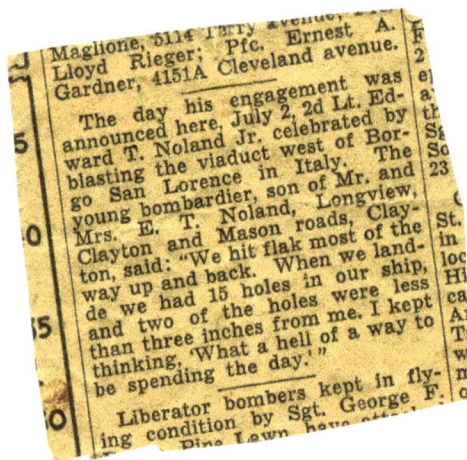

Newspaper clipping from the family archive. Original source unknown.

aviation."⁵) Tee then put his artistic talent to work and created what was called "nose art"—an illustration painted on the nose of the plane. The image Tee painted was of a "blonde bombshell" in a red one-piece bathing suit, which was apparently the way he had decided Miss Mitchell should look. His work was applauded by fellow flyboys, and he wound up

Tee paints Miss Mitchell on his B-25

painting nose art on several other planes—names like "Double Trouble" and art depicting caricatures like Mickey Mouse. He also added the names of the pilot and co-pilot beneath the windows of the cockpit. On the Miss Mitchell, he painted his own name at the base of the Plexiglas dome, and under that he added the line "Pat's Pulverizer." He'd chosen "Pat," no doubt, to honor the girl—who was, by then, the fiancé—that he'd left behind.

Tee wearing his goggles

Tee and some of the crew pose beside Miss Mitchell

The log book entries continued:

July 4th.

Today there are truly big fireworks. We were briefed at 6:45A.M. and charted our course for Villafranca (SE of Genoa) to blow up Nazi warehouses and a field hdqts. [Headquarters]. This meant flak again & 50 enemy fighters within 30 miles of target.

We all joked as we went to our planes. Takeoff scheduled for 8:00A.M. Three minutes of eight the mission was called off because of clouds over target (in case of clouds our alternate target would be supply depot & RR [railroad] marshalling yards at Pontiferno.)

July 5th (Mission 2)

This was the completion of the mission postponed on the 4th. The briefing took place at 5:15A.M., and aloft at 6:30A.M. The target tonight is RR marshalling yards & bridges at Villafranca due north of Corsica. We left Corsica with twelve Spits as cover and proceeded to Laverno. The weather was perfect with small white clouds drifting over the blue Mediterranean below. As we drew close to the coast, I once again climbed into [my] flak suit & helmet & started my search for the 70 enemy fighters in the vicinity and flak. We flew over beautiful country to the

IP [refers to "initial point"—a World War II abbreviation to indicate where the bombers began their initial bomb run[6]] and started our bomb run (still no flak thank God). After I had dropped my 4,300lbs. of bombs, we turned for home. The town and harbor of Spezia lay some ten air miles to our left, and we knew it was heavily defended. It seemed unbelievable to look in the harbor and see German boats there (one destroyer). As we neared the coastline, a single ack ack burst and puffed up about a thousand yds. [yards] to the left, then thirty more followed and were still farther away. I even laughed at the futility of their fire. Now the only worry was fighters and we soon got out of their range with our Spits far above.

We landed at 8:30A.M. and I thanked God for my second mission. (It is disheartening to come back looking for mail and find none). Now for a short night.

But things were about to get more difficult for the squadron. The next entry Tee made in his log described his third mission:

July 6th, 3 Mission
Briefing this morning at 6:30. At 8A.M. we were on our way north to enter Italy at the same place as last night, north of Laverno. By the time we reached the continent there

were none of our fighters in sight. (85 enemy planes reported in vicinity.) We proceeded over Villafranca to our IP at Monfestino. Our target was due north between Reggio & Modena, two miles east of Rubiera. There was considerable flak near Modena, which was visible ten miles away. We turned on the IP on time and I looked out the nose to our target, which was clearly visible twelve miles away. As before, our target was RR & highway bridges along supply route to Germans at Florence.

We passed over the German airdrome (where there were 35 ME109s reported) & saw no planes. One minute later it was bombs away. We circled back over our target two minutes later & the dust had blown east so we could see our damage. We completely demolished the 200' hwy. bridge & tore gaping holes in the double RR bridge, putting it completely out of use. We were all happy & headed for home. One hour later we arrived back at Corsica without seeing any fighters & nearest flak was ten miles away. This is my first view of the Po Valley & Genoa.

Three months later, Tee received "The Air Medal" for that mission. The accompanying certificate *[see Appendix I]* reads:

For meritorious achievement while
participating in aerial flight as
bombardier of a B-25 type aircraft
during an attack upon a highway and
a railroad bridge at Rubiera, Italy
on 6 July 1944. Lieutenant Noland's
proficiency in combat reflects great
credit upon himself and the Military.

The certificate was signed by John K. Kannon, Major General, USA Commanding, and was given to Tee ". . . by direction of the President, under the provisions of Army Regulation 600-45 as amended, and pursuant to authority vested in me by the Commanding General, Mediterranean Theater of Operations."

— Chapter 4 —

July 10th, 4th Mission

Briefing at 8:00A.M. In the air at 8:50.
Our target was a large RR [railroad]
marshaling yard at Cremona [Italy], 30
mi. SE of Milan. We entered the continent
about 15 mi. E. of Genoa, and proceeded
to Camogli (IP) due north. A good day for
bombing and no flak or enemy fighters. Went
into bomb run at 10:20. Bombs away, &
nothing to do but watch the hits. We blew
the hell out of the railyard and an oil storage
tank, too. Reached base at 12:00 noon.
Everything OK. No flak, no fighters.

July 11th, Mission 5

This is one of those bad days. Briefing at
7:00A.M. which meant getting up at 5:30.
Our target is Alessandria, south of Milan.
B-24s went in several days before, but
couldn't hit, so here we go with about 100

bombers & a wing of fighters. We knew this was important. The target—RR [railroad] yards with over 1700 cans of German supplies. This is another good day for bombing and we entered the coast of France without mishap at 10:05 A.M.—proceeded due north to Alba and started for target 30 mi. NE. I was in the lead wing of last box so I could see the other 36 bombs. They blew box cars all over the sky & blew out a RR bridge over Po River E. of town. We let 'em fly & at 150 ft. intervals our bombs walked right in to the only unbombed part. Mission was a swell success. Returned to base at 11:55 & once again no flak & no ME-109s. Happy day! Top turret gunner has a bad case of nerves so we will probably lose him. He told me as we climbed into the ship that he thought it was his last mission. This can get you easy enough. I ought to be home in another 65 missions. Oh well, maybe the war will be over by then.

Mission #6, July 12th

Briefing took place at 6:45 A.M. & for the third straight day we were heading into territory almost to the Alps. This time our target was two bridges & an ammunition dump. Took off at 8:10 and 1 hour later we were at rendezvous at Isle of Capria.

Headed for Southern France and entered the continent at Sestri–Lavante [Levante], E. of Genoa. From there we went to Castlefranco in Po Valley & turned for IP San Felice 30 miles due north. It was colder than the devil at 13,000 ft. in shirt sleeves, & enemy fighters were active here, having shot down a B-26 yesterday. Looking across the valley we could see the smoke screens the Jerries had laid to hide the target. Turned on our bomb run & it was impossible to see the bridges for smoke. Two minutes before bombing I had my eyes glued on the lead ship 100 ft. ahead & over us & the turret gunner called out "two fighters approaching from rt. [right] front." I couldn't look because I had to watch the lead ship as we all bomb on him, but I wondered if the fighters were ours or not & when he would start firing. We dropped our bombs & I looked for the fighters, but our own P-47s had chased them down. They were two ME-109s. We started for home, but the formation got off course at Villafranca [Villafranca Di Verona] & headed for Spezia (Germans have 45 flak guns here). We waited for them to turn & finally when the black smoke & crashing explosions rocked us all around, the formation broke up. Planes went in every direction trying to get out of the flak. I heard some of the fragments rip thru our ship & we started hunting for enemy fighters. We were 70 miles from the rest & our wing ships. After about 5 minutes we caught up with the rest & landed. Damage done amounted to only 3 holes: 2 in my compartment and a 6 inch one in the fuselage.

July 12th, 7th Mission

Briefed at 3:00P.M. Took off & headed for N. Italy to bomb R.R. Bridge & yards at Borgoforte. We had missed the day before. Followed same course as yesterday and started on bomb run with a heavy overcast over the entire valley. We dropped on the clouds and returned home without seeing any flak.

July 14th, 8 Mission

Briefing at 4:00P.M. to bomb munition factory at Villafranca. It was a beautiful evening as we started out north. When we reached the southern coast of Italy, the clouds were so heavy that the ground wasn't visible. We went in about 30 miles but couldn't get through the clouds, so we returned to Corsica about seven P.M. We got credit for this one because we had been over enemy territory for about half an hour. It suited me all right.

July 15th, 9th Mission

Briefing at 6:30A.M. for two German pontoon bridges [a temporary "floating" bridge, mostly used during emergencies or wartime7] 12 miles N. of Ferarra. We ran a gauntlet of A-9(s) [the winged, "improved" versions of Germany's A-4 missiles8] from the coast on, with flak on both sides. As we passed by Leghorn, we could see dust & fires from the battle going on the GRD [ground]. We had accurate flak across the mountains to Modena. As we turned on our bomb run, I could see the bridge our first box had bombed, & it was cut completely in half with about four hundred feet in the center gone. We hit ours & broke it into 3 pieces & it floated away. We had flak all of the way to the target & home but didn't receive any hits.

July 16th — 10th Mission

Another Sunday morning and up at 6:00 for a 7:00 briefing. Two weeks ago this morning I had my first mission. Our target [today] was a fuel dump, a viaduct & a dam. We took of at 8:00A.M. & headed N. Made landfall at 9:00A.M. at Sestri. Proceeded from there to Modena, then to San Felice & turned for target at Mantova. My box tore the viaduct apart with 18000 lbs. of bombs, and the other two boxes hit their target with the same amount. We hit moderately accurate flak N. of Reggio but weren't hit. Rest of trip was uneventful, & we got home at 12:00 noon. We were talking over [the] mission in my room & Pub. Rel. Off. [the public relations officer] heard me say that we got all three & ought to get 300% eff. [efficiency] and made a report that that statement would make a good story. We are all happy as we have flown more missions than other squadron in the European Theatre & we have destroyed 10 bridges, a dam, & dump in the last ten missions.

July ___, 11th Mission

the last ten missions.
July ___ , 11th Mission

Tee's log book stopped there, but the bombing did not. In fact, he soon earned an "Air Medal and One Silver Oak-Leaf Cluster." A letter from J.A. Ulio, Major General, The Adjutant General, of the U.S. War Department *[see Appendix J for a reproduction of the letter]* read that the awards were:

> "For meritorious achievement while participating as bombardier in attacks upon **** *[Tee's log—and from the certificate he had previously received—indicated that this area included Rubiera]*, Italy on 6 July 1944, **** *[Cremona]*, Italy on 10 July 1944, **** *[Alessandria]*, Italy on 11 July 1944, **** *[somewhere near Modena]*, Italy on 15 July 1944, **** *[unknown]*, Italy on 27 July 1944, and **** *[unknown]*, Italy on 1 August 1944. In contributing to these outstanding achievements in precision bombing, the personal courage, professional skill and devotion to duty displayed by Lieutenant Noland reflect highest credit upon the Military Service of the United States."

The Air Medal[9] was first established by president Franklin D. Roosevelt in 1942, and made retroactive to 1939. Awarded for meritorious achievement for participating in an aerial fighting, the medal had different criteria depending on where the recipient had been engaged. In the European Theatre, it was presented to the bomber, photographic reconnaissance, or observation crewmembers for five "sorties." Fighter pilots needed to have had ten sorties; individual pilots and air crewmen were presented with one Air Medal for each enemy aircraft that they succeeded in shooting down. In the Pacific areas, higher criteria were set, as the air fighting was not as heavy as in Europe.

Air Medal with Silver Oak-Leaf Cluster affixed.

The Silver Oak Leaf Cluster[10] is a small silver replica of a twig that contains four oak leaves and three acorns at the base by the stem. It is the equivalent of five bronze oak leaf clusters, and is used as a meritorious device to hold ribbons. In Tee's case, the silver oak-leaf cluster represented five additional Air Medals for each mission after 6 July 1944 that was cited.

Though not much further information about Tee's service time has been found, it has been documented that on a mission on 17 September 1944, somewhere in Italy, the B-25 Tee was in was attacked, and he was injured—an incident that earned him the Distinguished Flying Cross *[see Appendix J]*. At the same time that the notice was sent of his Air Medal and Silver Oak-Leaf Cluster, the citation for the Cross was given:

Distinguished Flying Cross medal

> "For extraordinary achievement while
> participating in aerial flight as
> bombardier of a B-25 type aircraft. On
> 7 September 1944, Lieutenant Noland flew
> in an attack upon an enemy troop and gun
> concentration near *****, Italy. Upon
> the commencement of the bomb run, shell
> fragments from intense anti-aircraft fire
> wounded Lieutenant Noland and hurled
> him from position. Quickly recovering
> himself, Lieutenant Noland, displaying
> upmost determination and professional
> skill, returned to his bomb sight and
> released his bombs with precision
> accuracy upon this vital objective. On
> more than fifty-five combat missions, his
> outstanding proficiency and steadfast

devotion to duty have reflected great
credit upon himself and the Armed Forces
of the United States."

Tee had been hit in the shoulder when they'd been hit by a barrage of flak, some of which went through the Plexiglas of his domed compartment. The fact that he righted himself, returned to his position, and released the bombs, is a testament to his courage, bravery, and the same kind of dedication to his work as he had to his family.

Tee in an undated photograph.

— Chapter 5 —

THE WAR CONTINUED. On 11 November 1944, Tee wrote to his sister Florence from Corsica *[see Appendix K]*:

My Dear Florence,

This is just a note to get you to do me a favor. I will wire or cable some money to you around the end of the month, and it should get there around the 15th of December. I would like for you to buy something for Pat & mail it to her, and buy something for Mom & Pop. There should be enough for something for Jane & Ed, too, and please take whatever is left and buy what you want from me. Don't be a nut about this now. I am asking you to do it and, by the time this reaches you the money will be cabled so there isn't much you can so about it. Just keep it under your hat. Thanks.

Here's something else just between the two of us. I think the end of my tour over here is in sight though still far away. Don't go guessing any time because you would be wrong. I would never tell you when I might be home because anything can happen . . . In the meantime don't spit in the wind & tell Andy hello for me. See you later. Be good.

All my love,
Tee

It was the last letter Florence would receive from her big brother.

The official Squadron History[11] for November 1944, reported several Mission Reports in which Tee participated:

- 4 November; Target: Magenta Road Bridge, Squadron Airplanes: Fourteen; Summary: No direct hits observed. Bombs dropped over and short of target. No other observations made.

- 5 November; Target: Cameri Road and Railroad Bridge; Squadron Airplanes: Six; Summary: Two runs made on target. Some bombs observed to walk across East end of bridge with possible direct hits. Other bombs fell over and to right of target. Flak: Scant, heavy inaccurate from target.

- 7 November; Peri Rail Full; Squadron Airplanes: Twelve; Summary: Crews report first box bombs dropped started short walking to, and through target. Two bombs seen to hit tracks. Second box bombs were over and East of target. Their box reports good concentration on tracks.

- 13 November; Target: Cittadell Rail Diversion Bridge; Squadron Airplanes: Twelve; Summary: Weather prevented attack.

- 16 November; Target: Citadella Railroad Diversion Bridge; Squadron Airplanes: twelve; Summary: Strings of bombs walked across center of Diversion Bridge with many D/H's [Direct Hits] observed. Other bombs hit NE approach. Center span observed down on breakway.

- 17 November; Target: Novska South Railroad bridge, Yugoslavia; Squadron Airplanes: Eight; Summary: Bombs straddled Center of Bridge. Other bombs fell over to SE. No bombs seen to hit bridge.

- 18 November; Target: Casarsa Railroad Diversion, Italy; Squadron Airplanes: Twelve; Summary: Good concentration on Diversion RR Bridge with probably D/H's. Other bombs overshot, hitting center of main RR bridge. Flak was moderate, heavy and accurate.

On 16 November 1944, the Squadron Diary—marked SECRET, but has since been declassified—for the 380th Bombardment Squadron (M), 310th Bombardment Group (M) AAF, APO #650 U.S. Army, reported noted the following:

```
The movie tonite was Louisiana Hayride
with Judy Canova. Some like this kind
of stuff and some don't. You take your
choice.
```

The following day, 17 November, this was recorded:

```
Mail came in and all seemed to have
letters. A few Xmas packages arrived.
```

No entry was made on 18 November. The next appeared the following day, 19 November, and read as if nothing disruptive had happened:

```
No mail today, although a few Xmas
packages did arrive for some to cheer
about.
```

On Thanksgiving Day, 23 November, this was cited:

```
. . . Plenty of turkey for everybody,
with stuffing and all the things that go
with it. Our meal was wonderful and all
appreciated the event. Plenty of mail
and Xmas packages, too. We did not have
a mission today, although we send out a
weather recce. The movie this evening
was "Song of the Road," with Charlie
McCarthy and Bergan, Bonite Granville,
and Sammy Kay's band.
```

The Squadron History also has a "Casualty Section." The entry for November 1944 reads:

```
WHILE PARTICIPATING IN AN OPERATIONAL
MISSION 18 NOVEMBER 1944 TO CARSARSA
RAIL DIVERSION AT C-150084, ITALY, THE
FOLLOWING NAMED OFFICERS AND ENLISTED
MEN ARE LISTED AS MISSING IN ACTION OVER
THE ABOVE NAMED TARGET:

Squadron airplanes: 12
```

P *[Pilot]* — 1st Lt. AT Ensley
CP *[Co-Pilot]* — 1st Lt. EV Ingram
B *[Bombardier]* —1st Lt. ET Noland
R *[Radio Operator]* — Sgt P Sorrent
G *[Gunner]* — S/Sgt DE Knott
TG *[Tail Gunner]* — TP Bango, S/Sgt

```
THIS PLANE WAS LAST SEEN IN A TIGHT
SPIRAL ON FIRE, DUE TO A DIRECT HIT FROM
```

FLAK, AND WAS SEEN TO CRASH IN THE RIVER
BED JUST NORTH OF TARGET. 5 CHUTES SEEN
TO OPEN AND FLOATED TO THE GROUND. NO
OTHER INFORMATION AVAILABLE.

It was later reported that Tee's plane was the "only casualty of the month."

Shortly after, Tee's parents received word that he was missing in action. The Army Air Corps also gave them Tee's belongings that he'd kept in Corsica: some cash* (from Italy, France, Egypt, and Algiers) that he kept in a leather folder, a photo of him "crossing the hump" (a term used when an airman crossed the treacherous Himalayan Mountains[12]), his log book, a German shaving mirror, and a German Panzer arm patch worn by those who served in German armored tanks.

Edward[4] refused to believe that Tee would not return.

"Short Snorter" - Ed Noland 12-29-43

Jesse W ...
John J. Hammerel
James E. Duegard
Newman W. Woolery

Some of Tee's bills were marked "Short Snorter." Research shows this was a term used when crew mates traditionally signed each other's bills to signify "good luck" when they crossed the Atlantic Ocean. Later, there were often drinking games, including when friends at a bar wanted a round ... and the mate with the fewest signatures on his "short snorter" had to pick up the tab.

Tee Noland's additional Short Snorter, front and back

Short Snorter Noland
Casablanca — 3-17-44

Walter S. Sherman
Albert O Hochnell Jr.
Richard Hyman
John Rougagaoc Jr.
Nathan Sherman
John J. Hammerstein
IL IL
Newman W. Woolery
Capt. John C. Meleracher

Additional currancey Tee had collected:

Algeria   *Italy*   *Morracco*

Algeria

Egypt

Tripoli

"WHAT HAVE YOU HEARD?" Florence asked the military man who, months later, appeared at the front door. She had seen him approach her parents' house; her husband, Andy, was with him. Andy was in the service, stationed in Texas at the time, so she knew something was wrong. She intercepted them before her parents realized they were there.

"What have *you* heard?" the man asked in reply.

"That my brother is missing," she said.

"Oh," he said.

And she knew then—by the somber look on Andy's face, and by the way the man had responded—that Tee had been killed.

The man with Andy turned out to be Lt. Art Ensley, Tee's friend, and the pilot of the plane on that fatal run. Tee's parents joined them; they all moved into the parlor, sat down, and Art told them what had happened.

"We were scheduled to hit a railyard in Modena . . ." he began. He told them how Tee had been waiting for transport back to the States, how Art had told Tee he was without a bombardier, how the mission was important, that they were to be the lead plane. He told them he'd asked Tee to go with them as a favor.

But the Germans had been ready for them. Just as Art zeroed in on the location, a burst of flak from below took out the B-25's hydraulics.

The tail gunner was killed instantly. Art made the call for everyone to bail out. But Tee had already readied the bombs to be deployed—he explained that this was not done until seconds before the bombs were to be released, in case the mission wound up being scrapped. Tee had shouted up to Art that they should jump; that he'd follow them right after he dropped the bombs. Seconds after the others parachuted out, Tee deployed the bombs . . . but the plane went down in flames before Tee could escape.

Of the four who parachuted (there had apparently not been five as the Squardon History had reported), the pilot and the co-pilot landed safely on the Italian side of the riverbed; the radio operator and the gunner landed on the German-occupied side. Art had a broken leg and a separated shoulder, but knew that he and his co-pilot had been lucky. The Italian Underground, sympathizers to the Allies, soon took them in. While their wounds were being tended to, Art and the co-pilot were routed to northern Italy then to Croatia, where other Underground members made contact with the Allies and arranged for a D-3 to fly into the woods and fly them out. Neither of them faced combat again.

"Early on," Art said, "Tee and I agreed that if we ever were shot down and one of us survived, the other one would go back and find the wreckage, and try to figure out what had happen to the one who didn't make it." Because Art was injured and unable to go himself, he had pleaded with the Underground to do it for him. They did.

Art then handed the Nolands Tee's belt buckle and his ID. He said the wreckage made it clear that, like the gunner, Tee had been killed instantly.

The proof seemed indisputable, but, Edward[4] still refused to believe that his son was dead.

Tee's belt buckle and ID

On 19 November 1945, a letter arrived *[see Appendix L]*. It was addressed to Tee's mother. By then, the family had moved out to the farm. The letter read in part:

> *Since your son, First Lieutenant Edward T. Noland, Jr., 01032468, Air Corps, was reported missing in action 18 November 1944, the War Department has ascertained hope that he survived and that information would be revealed dispelling the uncertainty surrounding his absence . . . he was a bombardier aboard a B-25 . . . which departed its base in Italy, 18 November 1944, on a combat mission to Casarsa, Italy. Casarsa is located on the Taliamento River in northeastern Italy, approximately forty-five miles north of Venice. At about 1:00p.m., while over the target, just after bombs had been released, the plane received a direct hit, which set the right engine on fire and disabled the ship. Other hits caused the ship to explode and as it went down on fire, it broke in two pieces and landed in the river at Casarsa where it burned. Your son was not one of those who parachuted to safety. . .*
>
> *The finding does not establish an actual or probably date of death; however, as required by law, it includes a presumptive date of death . . . this date has been set as 19 November 1945, the day following the expiration of twelve months of absence. . .*
>
> *I hope you may find sustaining comfort in the thought that the uncertainty with which war has surrounded the absence of your son has enhanced the honor of his service to his country and of his sacrifice."*

The letter was signed by Edward F. Witsell, Major General, Acting Adjutant General of the Army.

On 6 December 1945, First Lieutenant Edward[5] T. Noland, Jr. was posthumously awarded the Purple Heart *[see Appendix M]*, the award established by "General George Washington at Newburgh, New York, August 7, 1782 … for Military Merit and for Wounds received in action resulting in his death." He also received a posthumous declaration from President Harry S. Truman *[see Appendix N]*.

With the war then over, Edward[4] hired one of the private organizations that sent teams throughout the world-torn world to locate the remains of loved ones. The team found the wreckage of the plane: the dry riverbed had flooded in the spring; the task must have been difficult, but they succeeded. And Tee's remains were brought back to St. Louis.

On 8 July 1946, Tee's younger sister, Florence, gave birth to twins: a girl, named Barbara Adele Baur; a boy named Edward Turner Baur.

On 24 July 1949, Tee's older brother, Bob, and his wife Josephine had a baby boy: they named him Edward[6] Turner Noland.

By then, Edward[4]'s health had declined; he died on 11 December 1949. He was buried beside his son's remains in Valhalla Cemetery, St. Louis, Missouri. Their graves are marked with simple granite markers.

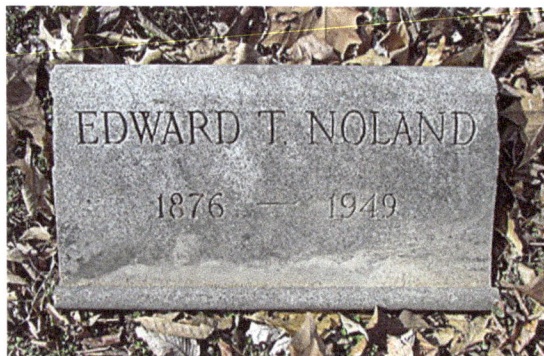

Cemetery markers of Edward[4] and Edward[5] from Find-a-Grave (www.findagrave.com).

— Epilogue —

"THEY WERE JUST A BUNCH OF YOUNG GUYS trying to do their part to end the war," Edward Noland Baur—now called "Uncle Tee"—has said.

Tee Baur, the first of whom became one of Tee's many namesakes, became determined to preserve his uncle's legacy, and the legacy of all United States WWII aviators. He became involved with the Commemorative Air Force, a group that had begun in 1957 with a mission to keep history alive. Tee learned that of nearly 10,000 B-25s that had been built, only 21 were still in existence. Many of the others had been retrofitted for use as cargo planes, crop dusters, or other purposes. But Tee set out to find one.

In 1982, he succeeded.

The CAF named his plane the "Show Me," after the State of Missouri's unofficial slogan. Tee Baur had a reproduction of a "lady" illustrated on the fuselage in a style similar to the way "1st Lt. Tee" had painted the Miss Mitchell. He had the names of the CAF pilot, Col. R. Bond, and the co-pilot, Col. F. Nedner, painted beneath the cockpit windows. Beneath the window of the nose he had painted: Lt. E. T. Noland, Jr. USAAF.

At the first reunion of the Commemorative Air Force that Tee attended in the 1990s, he was startled to see another B-25 that had been restored—one that bore the name "Miss Mitchell" and the illustration of the blonde "bombshell" in the one-piece red bathing suit on the fuselage. He quickly remembered that Tee had been shot down in an inventory plane, because the Miss Mitchell had gone in for repairs. He also had learned that she had flown until the end of the war.

As for the "Show Me" . . . Tee intends for the plane to keep flying until 2045, to mark the 100th anniversary of the "official" date of his uncle Tee's death.

Tee Baur

Edward Turner
Noland[7]

Tee Baur with
the original
"Miss Mitchell."

Tee Baur also connected with Art Ensley's daughter; and he was able, through the Freedom of Information Act,[13] to obtain previously CONFIDENTIAL documents. Among these were three statements taken on 21 November 1944 from fellow airmen who witnessed the crash. Due to the poor quality of the reproduction, the contents follow.

Submitted by: S/Sgt. Dennis Karraker *(sp.?)*:

The plane was hit while in about a 30º left bank and it started down straight at close to a 45º angle. One chute opened almost immediately, then another; there was a short delay then another opened. The plane made what looked like a right turn, then two more white objects floated out; then it plunged straight down into the crater of the river bed and burst into flames. The left engine was smoking and burning a little as it was going down.

Submitted by: 1st Lt. Albert H. Adams:

The following observations were made by myself and members of my crew on the mission of 18 November 1944 in connection with the loss of a plane on that mission:
The position in the formation was No. 6, flying left wing to the No. 4 ship which went down. About ten to fifteen seconds after the bombs were

released, my top turret gunner noticed
smoke pouring from the right engine of
the No. 4 ship. Approximately twenty to
thirty seconds after the bomb release,
flames were seen coming from both left
and right tanks. The plane, still under
control, nosed down slightly then
abruptly straight ahead. My bombardier
followed the ship all the way down to
the ground. He observed no parachutes
opening and no one getting out of the
burning plane. Three crew members
observed the burst of flak that hit
the ship and believe it to have hit
just forward of the right wing at the
juncture of the wing and fuselage.

Though the bombardier had the plane
in sight all the way down, he believes
it is very possible that he could have
missed seeing individuals leaving the
ship on a delayed jump since we were in
a climbing turn away from the falling
plane.

Submitted by: T/Sgt. Byron F. Link:

The following observations were
made by myself on the mission of 18
November 1944 on which one airplane was
lost.

At about 10 to 15 seconds after
bombs were away, I notice(d) number four
plane start smoking and flames coming

out of the bomb-bay doors, suddenly the
plane nosed down for about 5000 feet
then seemed to straighten out and I
observed one chute blossom out, then the
plane started to move almost straight
down again and hit in the center of the
river bed. After I saw it crash I again
looked for the chute and this time I
noticed the second one, so I believe two
of the men to have gotten out.

Another previously CONFIDENTIAL document received was the
MISSING AIR CREW REPORT. Although most of it is technical,
one section is quite clear:

NUMBER OF PERSONS ABOARD AIRCRAFT: 6

Below that is the list of the crew members and their status. It is
unknown when this report was filled out, though it might have been
at the same time the previous statements were given. Of the six crew
members, only five names were listed; the sixth might have appeared
on the reverse side of the report, but had not been included. Along with
their serial numbers, the names read:

1. Pilot   Ensley, Arthur T.   1st Lt.   MIA
2. Co-Pilot   Ingram, Elden V.   1st Lt.   MIA
3. Bombardier   Noland, Edward T., Jr.   1st Lt.   MIA
4. Radio-*[illegible]* Sorrenti, Pasquale Sgt.   MIA
5. Turret Gunner Knott, Donald   S/Sgt.   MIA
   [Tail Gunner S/Sgt. Bango's name was missing.]

Hand-written, obviously added at a later date, were notations next to the MIA status of crew members 1. (Ensley), 2. (Ingram), and 4. (Sorrenti). The notation read: RTD *[Returned to Duty]*. There is no notation made for crew member 5. (Knott); but for 3. (Noland), there is a small "o."

In addition, three INDIVIDUAL CASUALTY QUESTIONNAIRE copies were received. It is unclear when these were typed, but one separate sheet that came with it indicates that the forms were filled by the plane's pilot, 1st Lt. Arthur Ensley. However, on the report about Tee, the co-pilot's name (1st Lt. Elden V. Ingram) and address are hand-written; we do not know if that is Ingram's signature, in which case it may indicate he was the one who filled out the questionnaire. Either way, it indicates that Art Ensley had not been with his co-pilot when rescued.

Legible sections of the contents read:

Name of Crew Member:
S/Sgt. Thomas P. Bango

Was he injured:
Yes. Four pieces of flak about half the size of a penny, two in his left shoulder, two in left leg just below the knee.

Any explanation of his fate based in part or wholly on supposition:
I was with Sgt. Bango for about eight days after we were shot down, we were at Tremonti, Italy with intelligence personnel and the Italian Partisians. The Germans started to fight with the partisians in that area so I started walking out. Sgt. Bango could not walk

yet due to the wound in his leg. He was supposed to have been taken farther back into the mountains w(h)ere it was supposed to have been sa(f)er from the Germans. I have not heard anything about him since.

Name of Crew Member:
S/Sgt. Donald H. Knott

Last contact or conversation just prior to or at time of loss of plane:
I saw Sgt. Knott just as the plane burst into flames.

Was he injured:
I believe he was, as he got out of the turret just as the plane burst into flame(s).

Where was he last seen:
Turret compartment.

Any heresay information:
One man believed to have been in the plane when it crashed, one man's parachute didn't open, and one man believed to have been taken prisoner.

Source:
The Italians helped me.

Any explanation of his fate based in part of wholly on supposition:

Have none due to the fact that I have never seen or heard from 3 of the members of the crew & I do not rely to(o) much on heresay information.

Name of Crew Member:
1st Lt. Edward T. Noland, Jr.

Did he bail out:
Not known.

Last contact just prior to or at time of loss of plane:
Last contact Bombardier dropped bombs on target.

Was he injured:
Not known.

Where was he last seen:
Bombardiers Compartment.

Any heresay information:
One man believed to have been in the plane when it crashed, one man's parachute didn't open, one man believed to have been taken prisoner.

Source:
The Italians who helped me out.

Any explanation of his fate based in part or wholly on supposition:
Have none due to the fact I have never

```
seen or heard from 3 of the members of
the crew & I do not rely to(o) much on
heresay.
```

Although these reports seem somewhat inconsistent with others, one fact couldn't be doubted: 1st Lt. Edward[5] Turner Noland, Jr. had served his country, and served it well.

— ENDNOTES —

1. Advertising Age "Liggett & Myers Tobacco Co." 15 September 2003.

2. www.fold3.com/page/286264074_edward_t_noland/stories/

3. www.pacificaviationmuseum.org/aircraft/B25b — There is some discrepancy here, as some research indicated the bomb capacity was 4,000 lbs., and others record 5,000 lbs. Apparently variations were frequently manufactured.

4. www.historynet.com/world-war-ii-north-africa-campaign.htm

5. https://en.wikipedia.org/wiki/North_American_B-25_Mitchell

6. www.warbirdsresourcegroup.org/URG/glossary.html

7. www.britannica.com/technology/pontoon-bridge

8. www.aeroflight.co.uk/military/a9_missile.htm

9. https://en.wikipedia.org/wiki/Air_Medal

10. https://en.wikipedia.org/wiki/Oak_leaf_cluster

11. http://57thbombwing.com/380th_History/19441101_19441130.pdf

12. https://warisboring.com/the-hump-was-the-deadliest-cargo-flight -in-history-13fe4ff5a09#.dckm04qbn

13. www.foia.gov

— APPENDIX A —

7 December 1943 Letter from Tee to his sister Florence

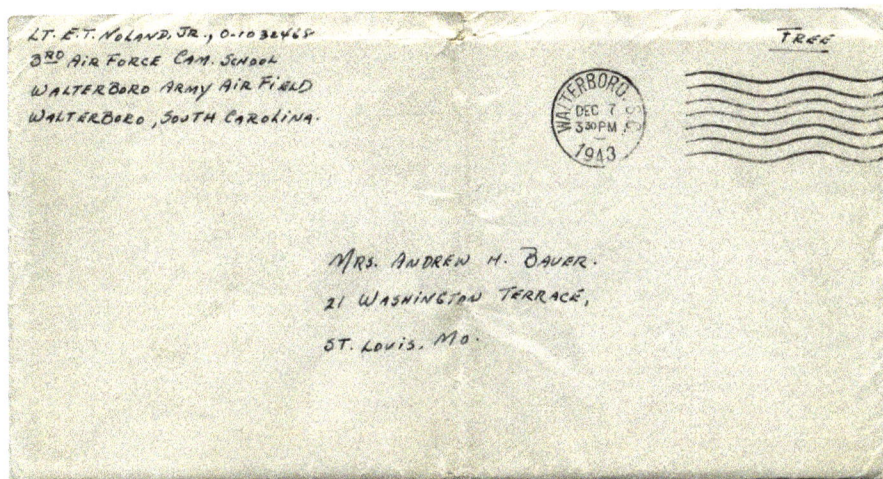

LT. E.T. NOLAND, JR., 0-1032468
3RD AIR FORCE CAM. SCHOOL
WALTERBORO ARMY AIR FIELD
WALTERBORO, SOUTH CAROLINA.

TREE

WALTERBORO
DEC 7
3:30 PM
1943

MRS. ANDREW H. BAUER.
21 WASHINGTON TERRACE,
ST. LOUIS, MO.

U.S. ARMY | AIR FORCES

Monday Night.

Dear Florence.

You sure gave me a fist full of the
latest news in your last letter. First of all.
Mother had written to me about Aunt Bess
being very ill, and I am very sorry to
hear that she is so sick. I know Dad
must be very worried because she is one
of our favorites and I think Dad liked her
a little more than his other sisters If
there is anything I can do to help let me
know right away. I wish it was possible
for me to be there, because I feel that having
us around, or knowing we were there would
help her to get well quicker. She has always
been my favorite aunt. I hope by the time
you receive this, she is much better. I will

write to her when she is well enough.

The second thing — no Andy didn't tell me anything about you raising a family, but I think it is fine, and when I remember how fond you always were of babies and dolls, there is no doubt in my mind as to how happy you will be. I guess it looks pretty much as though I'm the cow's tail in the family, or the gape's nose, but I am not sorry I haven't advanced with the rest of the family. It is true, there have been a thousand times in the past five years that made me feel as though I had nothing, no matter how much I was making, I had nothing of my own that couldn't be bought. Even now, when I feel I definitely have something, and am making more money than ever and saving over $100.00 a month, when my work is finished in the evening, you begin to look for something to do until morning such as going to the show or playing cards. No

U.S. ARMY AIR FORCES

matter where you go or how many shows you
see, there is still the feeling that you aren't
really happy. No I don't regret waiting this
long because I feel that what I have
found is well worth the waiting. I am
very happy, knowing how you _and I_
have both felt about the other kids in the
family in their choice of companions.
that you feel as though you will like
Pat. I am sure you will because she
is really a swell girl. I sincerely believe
that to her, I am more important than
anything, and to know she feels that way
is a big consolation. I would be very
happy to have you write to her whenever
you can. Anything you want to say is O.K.

Mother was after me about having a picture made when I was home, but I didn't do it until I hit N.C. I think one of them (the big one) is all right, but the two small ones — not so hot. I will mail them all home, but since I will not be there Christmas, wrap the big one up for me and give it to Mother for me. I can't buy her dishes or silver that she doesn't already have.

Since the baby is a 50-50 proposition, tell Andy I think it's fine. You are both very fortunate, but you deserve to be.

Here is Pat's address if you should want to write to her. PAT SHRERTZ, 521 E FILMORE, HARLINGEN, TEXAS. Drop me a line when you have time (before the 18th as I return to Raleigh that day). Congratulations again to both of you and tell the family hello for me.

Love to all of you,
Lee.

31 January 1944 Letter from Tee to his sister Jane

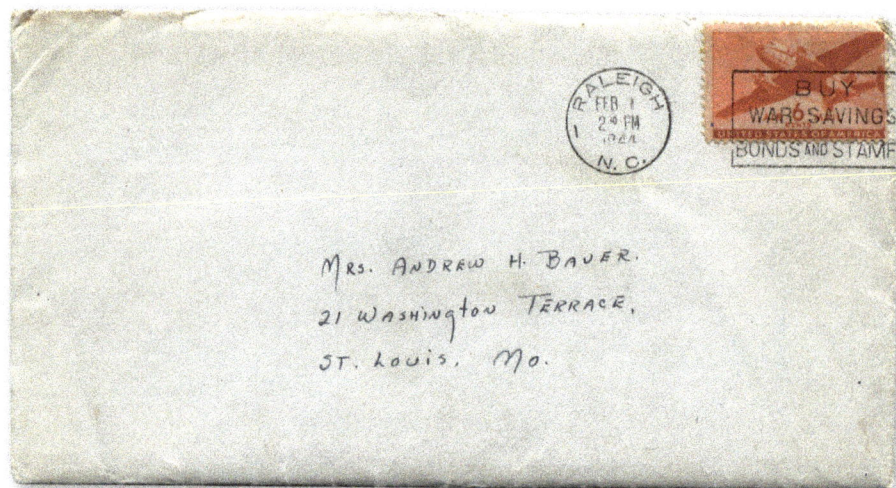

RALEIGH
FEB 1
2⁴ PM
1944
N.C.

BUY
WAR SAVINGS
UNITED STATES OF AMERICA
BONDS AND STAMP

Mrs. Andrew H. Bauer.
21 Washington Terrace,
St. Louis, Mo.

Edward T. Noland
Army of the United States

January 31st.

Dear Dad & Florence, & Andy.

I managed to get up to Morgantown for a day this past week end, and everything seems to be fine. From all I could gather, they are expecting all sorts of things around the last of this week. I know they will be glad when it is all over, although they say they have never lost a father yet. I thought Mother stood the trip very well and I think she is having a good time. I know Betty wouldn't take anything for having her there.

On my way back, I stopped at the Statler Hotel in Washington for supper

between planes. They were having the
President's birthday ball that night. I
sat the next to Madeline Carroll in the
lobby for about ten minutes without
knowing it. She's a little older than her
pictures show her to be. Washington is
a very pretty place, but I would never
want to live there.

We should finally get away from
here around the last of this week.
We are all about worn out waiting.

Tell Florence I am still waiting
for her to write to Pat.

I saw Mrs. Buchanan today and
she invited me to her house for supper.
She also asked to be remembered to all
of you. She and Mary Cameron are the
pick of that family. I can't see them now
because they ask so many questions I can't

Edward T. Noland
Army of the United States

answer.

I looked all over Washington to get a gold charm for Florence's bracelet but I didn't have any luck. I'll keep on looking.

Dad call John Butler around the tenth of the month to find out for me if he received a check for $150.00 from the government for my account. I have allotted everything but my flying pay and foreign duty pay to my account so he should receive it every month.

I must get to bed. Take care of yourselves & tell Andy I received his letter but I haven't had time to answer it.

I will write again before I leave and give you the final low down. Be good and when I get back we will have some fun, *after* I get married which will be the first day I am back. I'm tired of living among men and by myself.

all my love to all of you,

Lee.

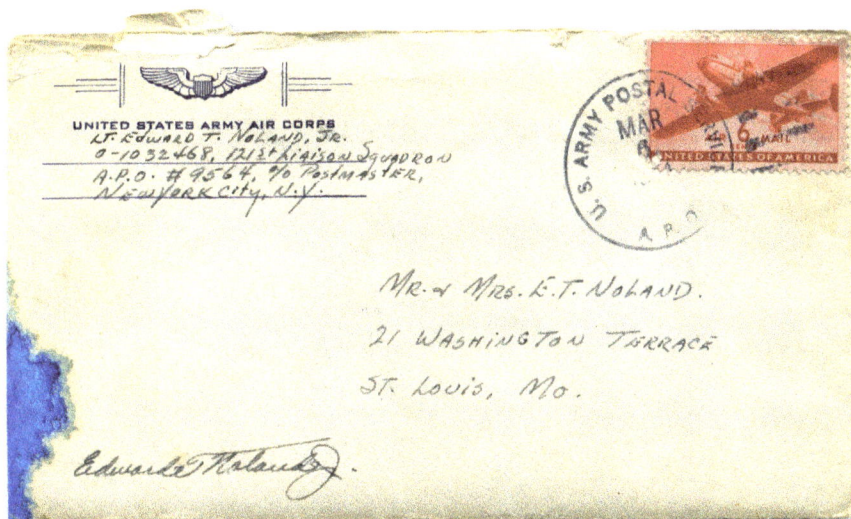

UNITED STATES ARMY AIR CORPS
Lt. Edward T. Noland, Jr.
O-1032468, 1213th Liaison Squadron
A.P.O. #9564, % Postmaster,
New York City, N.Y.

Mr. & Mrs. E.T. Noland.
21 Washington Terrace
St. Louis, Mo.

Edward T. Noland Jr.

UNITED STATES ARMY AIR CORPS

Saturday Night.
March 4th

Dear Mother, Dad & Florence.

I was very glad to be able to talk to you last night. It sounded pretty good to me to hear all of you. When I get home I will tell you all about my call. I do wish that Nancy had more to say than just hello or so. You could have knocked me over with a feather when Dad told me it was Nancy. The only thing wrong with calling up is the minute I get you on the phone, everyone says hello & goodbye in the same breath.

I was glad Mrs. Jones got her letter to Zach before he went to New York. He was probably very surprised that I had called.

I tried to allott fifty of the $100.00
I am drawing a month for bonds,
but we can't allott our flight pay
so that put the screws on that. I
wanted to send the bonds to Pat,
but no soap.

When you see Mrs. Smith, tell
her to ask Johnson to drop me a
line. You can give him my address.

Well in one month & a half
you will be moving to the country,
and the last of May I would have
been married. It seemed far away
~~in December when I told you of~~
my plans, but it seems much
farther away now, except that I
feel everything is set and OK. Just a
matter of time, and believe me, from
one who knows, it means an awful
lot to know everything is perfect. If
you remember correctly, the other

UNITED STATES ARMY AIR CORPS

time I thought I might get married,
I was never positive, and now
I am glad I didn't because Pat is
a thousand times more ideal.

You will find her relatively
inexperienced and actually a young
girl, but anything I want is what
she wants, and I guess from her
letters to me she feels the sun
rises and sets on me, so that
makes her just what I want along
with everything else she has. You
would die at her last letter. She
said she hoped we would have
five sons and a daughter or two,
but boys are her main wish.
She is actually terribly young and I
am glad of it. I am nine years older

than she is, but she knows what she
wants and has wonderful taste in
clothes and everything (including
men! ahem!). This sounds very
much as though I am trying to sell
her to you and I'm not. You'll like
her and realize she's good for me
without that.

Tell Pop not to get too rambunctious
on the farm, and for Pete's sake
take care of yourselves. I hope
Florence & Andy have the kind
of baby they want. Give my love
to Betty when you see her. I still
can't see Art, but I don't have to.

Write when you can, as I
sure like to get your letters. Everything
is fine. Be good. Tell Andy "hi"!
                    Love to Everyone,
                        Bee.

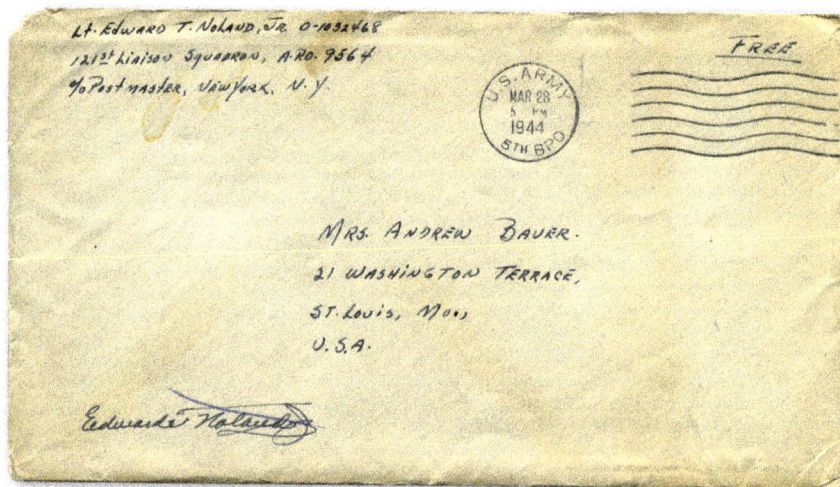

Somewhere in North Africa
March 27th, 1944.

Dear Florence.

I suppose that by this time, you
are not having too much fun or liberty,
but knowing how you have always been
about children, I am sure you can
hardly wait until you have yours. I
am sure it won't matter to you whether
it is a boy or a girl. I am not any
too much help being here, but if I was
there I couldn't do a thing but worry
while you did the wash. After almost
a year of active flying, we 'sweat it out'
when one of us is in a jam and we
can't help them. When you go into the
hospital, remember you have a brother
someplace over here that won't be too
busy to think of you then, and I shall
worry about it until I hear that everything

is all right.

I have looked all over two towns for some sort of a trinket for you and Betty and Jane, but there is absolutely nothing that is worth having. Most of the stuff they call sterling is stamped pewter. One of the boys bought a terrible looking handkerchief today for two hundred francs (four dollars). It wasn't even nice enough to bother to say it came from Africa. In the event I find anything, I will send it to you.

By the way, I hope the family didn't drop over when I asked either you or Mother to select a ring for Pat. I couldn't possibly get one, much less get around a decent jewelry store. I should have around seven hundred dollars by June to buy her ring. If that isn't enough, get it anyhow and let me know how much more you need. I will have it with me.

The weather hasn't changed. It is still awfully hot all day and cold as the devil at night. I am living in a tent. Our showers are about ½ a mile away and we walk there every day.

Dad will probably have an awfully ~~hard time getting used to not working,~~ but he will enjoy himself when he learns how to just mess around.

I believe I will have my own plane when I finally reach my destination. It will sure be a relief. You can send me any film you can for my camera because I can't get any here. If I get any good shots which are not taboo, I will send them to you.

This will probably be my last letter to you before you go to the hospital, so remember I'm holding my thumbs. I still haven't received any mail, but I can wait as long as I will get it later. Tell Mother & Dad & Curly hi!

Love to Everyone,
Lee!

90

— APPENDIX E —
7 May 1944 Letter from Tee to his sister Jane

May 7th, 1944.
North Africa.

Dear Jane,

I am not quite certain as to Ed's status at the time of this writing. I hope for his sake that his commission in the Navy came thru. He will be much better off than in the army. I wouldn't trade, but I am a little younger than Ed and I am a little more used to not counting definitely on anything.

I was very sorry to hear about Mindy having the measles, but I guess they all get them. Lord only knows if that is all he gets growing up he won't be a boy. Jane I sure hope you move out with the family if Ed goes into the army or navy. It would mean an awful lot to Dad & Mom.

I have never told them, but one of the things
that has always hurt me whenever I came
home on a leave is how lonesome they
both are. It hurt just sitting at the dinner
table with them and realizing they are
finally alone. Of course I know it must be
but mark my words, they will live a
happier life with you and Florence with
them. I intend to spend all of my
leave with them when I get back, except
about five days when I am married. I
have no desire to go away then but it will
take me some time to get used to a
different living & I know it will be
easier for Pat too, and I want to see an
awful lot of her after this. Must get to bed.
Thanks for writing and keep it up. You have
all been swell to me. I am enclosing a
picture of Pat. Please give it to Mother. Take
care of everybody.

all my love,
Bill

May 14th, 1944.
North Africa.

Dear Florence.

Congratulations!! I knew it would be a
boy but I didn't want to get your hopes up
too high. I sure am glad you didn't have
too much trouble or pain. I know Curley
must be very happy. He certainly should
be.

I received your letter written on May 3rd
this evening and you certainly seemed
to be well enough. I knew you are
about to go nuts with joy. I am glad
it is over with. In a couple of more
weeks you will almost be back to normal.
I can see you and Betty fighting over
the tub to see who gets to wash diapers
first.

My information is a little low at this

paint so I'll have to ask you to show the
letter. Tell dad I received his letter and also
the one from Vic Sundequist. He and I.
roomed together at Brooks and Harlingen
and I was glad to hear from him. He was
in New Georgia at the time of his letter.

My duties are entirely disassociated with
my old ones. I am in an entirely different
outfit. I would tell you all about it
except that everyone would think up a
hundred new worries. I will tell you
this much, I am not in four motored
bombers so Mother ought to be glad because
she said she didn't like them. I am
in a bombardment squadron and have
been flying around three hours a day.
For your added info. they don't have
commissioned gunners except for teaching
so I'm not a gunner. Have all you have

to do is think of my training in Texas, look at the type of outfit I am in and you can see what I'm doing. That's right! Bombing! How else do you suppose I knew where Geo. Steward is? Since you finally know what I'm doing, I will add to it by saying that I hope I will get my missions in quick and the war will be over soon because I am awfully anxious to get back. As for what I am going to do when the war is over, I don't know, and it will mean that I will be married long before then, but I just plain don't care to blow any bubbles about that this far ahead.

I guess you are all moved by now. I wish I could have been there to help & cuss about it. I would have had fun.

Tell Mother I had a very nice letter from Jane telling me all about Windy and I know Ed is relieved that things are finally settled one way or the other. Of course I knew Jack F. was dead. I was looking for his grave to take a picture of it for Ed and his mother. I will find it before I come back now that I know where it is.

So much for now. I think it's swell you have a boy. Give Mom + Dad + Nancy and Windy all my love. You are all swell. I love all of you very much (of course Pat is a little different kind of love). Don't worry about me because everything is and will be fine. We had one hell of a sandstorm last night, but today was perfect. Must get to bed. Goodnight to everyone.

all my love,
Bee.

May 31st, 1944.
North Africa.

My Dear Florence.

I am very happy to hear the Junior is doing
so well, and that you are getting along fine. Your
last V mail has started me wondering a little
bit about something. So I'll have to tell you
just in case I am right, there will be someone
there who understands — no —

Sometime ago, before Easter, I wrote Bob
and Jo a note in which I told them that
in the event I should not get back to the
states, and if the family was informed I
was missing in action, then (and then only)
I wanted them to name their first boy after
dad for me. I have wondered a little about
how far he would go on a lot of things where
mother & dad were concerned, and I must
admit I don't know. This is strictly between
you and me. I don't mind if you tell Andy, but

under no circumstances, unless he should try. Are Mother and dad to know the contents of this letter. I would rather not having Mother worrying about me not getting back. I can't stop Pat from worrying, but Mother has enough others + not as much spare time as Pat.

This is an odd letter. I know that too, but I would prosecute him if he should do anything like that, and I would hate to change his kid's name, but I would. I feel I could trust you and Andy to do anything for me otherwise I would never have mentioned this to anyone. So much for this!

It is hotter than hell here and no shade of any kind. We don't have any trouble keeping cool at night though.

I flew a mission this morning as copilot on a B-25 and it was a lot of fun.

Pat told me in her last letter she had gotten a toy for the baby. I am glad you liked it. Tomorrow is pay day and I'll draw four hundred and eleven dollars for this month. Not bad for a young fellow!

Well I got to close for now. Be good squirt!
Take care of the family for me, and I'll be
back, soon I hope!! The sooner the quicker
There isn't anymore news, so I will
have to stop. Tell Jane & Ed hello for me. I hope
Andy is still at Scott Field. Glad Push is doing
fine. She's a real dog. I wish I had a picture
of her. So long for now ————

all my Love
Lee.

Book No. 1.

— Combat Record —
Edward T. Noland Jr.
380th Bombardment Squadron,
310th Bombardment Group.

The following experiences
in the War with Germany
are my own, and I start
this record in Ghissonachia,
Corsica, July 2nd, 1944
after serving two years
and eleven months in the
U.S. Army Air Forces —
All accounts of ensuing
missions are written after
the Bombing as no personal
posessions go with us lest it
be harmful if we are shot down

As an afterthought, I
should like to add that
my main worry was
whether I would receive
any mail from Pat or
from home. At the
completion of every
mission the let down from
anticipation, worry &
excitement is so
strenuous that we all
usually slept for several
hours.

Sunday, July 2nd, 8am.
This is my first bomb
mission, and I fully realize
I know nothing of war. The
feeling before takeoff is very
similiar to the tension before
a football game.
At 8am we climbed in
our B-25 and started the
engines. At eight twenty we,
with the rest of our Sqdn.
are airborne. The target
is a vital viaduct NE of
Florence, Italy which the
germans are using as a
supply route. We crossed
the blue waterof Gurian
Sea and into Allied held

Italy 3 miles N. of Talamone.
We proceeded (after one
crew member hollered ladies
& gents, this is Italy) to
Foligno where we turned
North into German held
territory. It looked the
same as any other to
me on this Sunday until
5 minutes later when I
saw a black burst of
the filthiest color imaginable. This was the first
Flak I have ever seen.
During the next twenty
minutes we dodged and
wove in and out of these
bursts, and I hurriedly
put on my flak vest &

helmet, at the same time
looking at our other ships
with black bursting all
around us. We ran thru
the puffs and explosions
of the 88mm. shells shook
the Mitchells like dead
leaves. So far everything
was live. We arrived at
Appechio for our next
change of course & headed
for Dicomanu to the
North. The Flak grew more
intense and the tail
gunner shouted 'for Christs
sake get out of here.'
I felt the same. You

simply sit and wait for the fragments to hit. We had not long to wait for in the next two minutes we were hit by five pieces but not damaged out side of holes. The rest of our formation took it too, and as I sat there with all the glass around me I prayed to come out all right. We had been told there would be FW 190s & ME 109s but none got close as our Spitfire cover kept them away. We finally flew over our Initial Point to begin our

Bomb run on BORGO, SAN LORENZO. Three minutes later I watched the bombay doors swing open on the lead ship and all of the others. Twenty seconds later we released our 4000 lbs. (per ship) of bombs and banked away. I have never before seen such an explosion & columns of smoke & dust.

We were half way through & on our way home through the same gauntlet of ack ack. There were deafening roars when the big shells burst around

us. Shortly afterward I felt a pain in my left shoulder and looked at the plexiglass overhead. There were two holes and two more about two inches wide through the floor. The shattering glass had hit me on the shoulder (no damage) & the flak passed about 3 inches from me on it way through. We called the gunners & radio operator and found them OK & I thanked God for his help.

We flew for about fifteen minutes more to our part of Italy &

home the same route.

When we landed we counted 15 flak holes in our ship, and I said to myself "I've had it!" I felt like a member of the team now. My first successful mission.

July 4th.

Today there are truely big fireworks. We were briefed at 6:45 AM and charted our course for VILLAFRANCA (SE of GENOA) to blow up Nazi warehouses and a field hdqts. This meant flak again & 50 enemy fighters within 30 miles of target.

We all joked as we went to our planes. Takeoff scheduled for 8:00 AM. Three minutes of flight the mission was called of because of clouds over target. (In case of clouds our alternate target would be supply depot & RR marshalling yards at PONTIFERNO).

July 5th (Mission 2)

This was the completion of the mission postponed on the 4th. The briefing took place at 5:15 P.M., and aloft at 6:30 P.M. The target tonight is R.R. marshalling yards & bridges at VILLAFRANCA due NORTH of

CORSICA. We left Corsica with twelve Spits as cover and proceeded to LAVERNO. The weather was perfect with small white clouds drifting over the blue MEDITERRANEN below. As we drew close to the coast, I once again climbed into flak suit & helmet & started my search for the 70 enemy fighters in the vicinity & flak. We flew over beautiful country to the I P & started our bomb run (still no flak thank God). After I had dropped my 4300 lbs. of bombs, we turned for home. The town & harbor of SPEZIA lay some ten air miles to our left, and we knew it was heavily defended. It seemed unachievable to look in the harbor & see German boats there (1 destroyer) As we neared the coastline, a single ack ack burst puffed up about a thousand yds. to the left. Then thirty more followed & were still farther away. I even laughed at the futility of their fire. Now the only worry was fighters & we soon got out of their range with our Spits far above. We landed at 8:30 P.M. & I thanked God for my second mission. (It is disheartening to come back looking for mail & find none). Now for a short night.

July 6th Mission.

Briefing this morning at 6:30. At 8:00 we were on our way North to enter Italy at the same place as last night, North of Laverno. By the time we reached the continent there were none of our fighters in sight. (85 enemy planes reported in vicinity) We proceeded over Villafranca to our IP at Montestino. Our target was due North between Reggio & Modena, two miles east of Rubiera. There was considerable flak near Modena which was visible ten miles away. We turned on the IP on time & I looked out the nose to our target which was clearly visible twelve miles away. As before, our target was RR. &

Highway bridges along supply route to Germans at Florence. We passed over the German airdrome (where there were 35 ME 109s reported) & saw no planes. One minute later it was bombs away. We circled back over our target two minutes later & the dust had blown East so we could see our damage. We completely demolished the 200' hiwg bridge & tore gaping holes in the double R.R. bridge putting it completely out of use. We were all happy & headed for home. One hour later we arrived back at Corsica without seeing any fighters & nearest flak was ten miles away. This is my first view of the Po Valley & Genoa.

July 10th, 4th Mission

Briefing at 5:00 AM. In the air at 8:00. Our target was a large RR marshalling yard at Cremona, 30mi. SE of Milan. We entered the continent about 15mi. E. of Genoa, and proceeded to Comegli (IP) due North. A good day for bombing and no flak or enemy fighters. Went into bomb run at 10:30. Bombs away. & nothing to do but watch the hits. We blew the hell out of the railyard & an old storage tank too. Reached base at 12:00 noon. Everything OK. No flak, no fighters.

July 11th. Mission 5

This is one of those bad days. Briefing at 7:00 am which meant getting up at 5:30. Our target is Alessandria south of Milan. B-24s went in several days before, but couldn't hit, so here we go with about 100 bombers & a wing of fighters. We knew this was important. The target- RR. yards with over 1700 cars of german supplies. This is another good day for bombing and we entered the coast of France without mishap at 10:05 a.m. proceeded due North to Alba and started for target 30 mi. NE. I was in the lead wing of last box so I could see the other 36

bombs. They blew box cars all over the sky & blew out a RR bridge over Po River E. of town. We let em fly & at 150ft. intervals our bombs walked right in to the only unbombed part. Mission was a swell success. Returned to base at 11:55 & over again no flak & no ME 109s. Happy day! Top turret gunner has a bad case of nerves so we will probably lose him. He told me as we climbed into the ship that he thought it was his last mission. This can get you easy enough. I ought to be home in another 65 missions. oh well, maybe the war will be over with then.

Mission #6, July 12th

Briefing took place at 6:45 A.M. & for the third straight day we were heading into territory almost to the Alps. This time our target was two bridges & an ammunition dump. Took off at 8:00 & 1 hour later were at rendevous at Isle of Caprio. Headed for Southern France & entered the continent at Sestri-Lavante, E. of Genoa. From there we went to CastleFranco in Po Valley & turned for IP San Felice 30 miles due North. It was colder than the devil at 13000 ft. in shirt sleeves, & enemy fighters were active here, having shot down a B-26 yesterday. Looking across the valley we could see the smoke screens the Jerries had laid to hide the target. Turned on our bomb run & it was impossible to see the bridges for smoke. Two minutes before bombing I had my eyes glued on the lead ship 100 ft. ahead & over us & the turret gunner called out two fighters approaching from rt. front. I couldn't look because I had to watch the lead ship as we all bomb on him, but I wondered if the fighters were ours or not & when he would start firing. We dropped our bombs & I looked for the

fighters, but our own P-47s had chased them down. They were two Me-109s. We started for home, but the formation got off course at Villafranca & headed for Spezia (Germans have 45 flak guns here). We waited for them to turn & finally when the black smoke & crashing explosions rocked us all around the formation broke up. Planes went every direction trying to get out of the flak. I heard some of the fragments rip thru our ship & we started hunting for enemy fighters. We were 30 miles from the rest & our wing ships. After about 5 minutes we caught up with the rest & landed. Damage done amounted to only 3 holes: 2 in my compartment & a 6 inch one in the fuselage.

July 13th, 7th Mission.

Briefed at 3:00 P.M. Took off & headed for N. Italy to bomb R.R. bridge & yards at Borgoforte. We had missed the day before. Followed same course as yesterday, and started on bomb run with a heavy overcast over the entire valley. We dropped on the clouds & returned home without seeing any flak.

July - 14th, 8 Mission

Briefing at 4:00 P.M. to bomb munition factory at Villafranca

It was a beautiful evening as we started out North. When we reached the southern coast of Italy, the clouds were so heavy that the ground wasn't visible. We went in about 30 miles but couldn't get through the clouds, so we returned to Corsica about seven P.M. We got credit for this one because we had been over enemy territory for about a half an hour. It suited me all right.

July 16th, 9th Mission.

Briefing at 6:30 A.M. for two German pontoon bridges 12 miles N. of Ferarra. We ran a gauntlet of A.A. from the coast on with flak on both sides. As we passed by Leghorn, we could see dust & fires from the battle going on there. We had accurate flak across the mountains to Modena. As we turned on our bomb run, I could see the bridge our first box had bombed, & it was cut completely in half with about four hundred feet in the center gone. We hit ours & broke it into 3 pieces & it floated away. We had flak all of the way to the target & home but didn't receive any hits.

July 16th - 10th Mission

Another Sunday morning &
up at 6:00 for 7:00 briefing.
Two weeks ago this morning
I had my first mission.
our Target was a fuel
dump, a viaduct & a
dam. We took off at 8:00
am & headed N. Made
landfall at 9:00 am at
SESTRI. Proceeded from there
to MODERNA, then to SAN
FELICE & turned for target
at MANTOVA. My box tore
the viaduct apart with
18000 lbs. of bombs, and the
other two boxes hit their

target with the same
amount. We hit moderately
accurate flak N. of Reggio
but weren't hit. Rest of
trip was uneventful, & we
got home at 12 noon.
We were talking over mission
in my room & Pub. Rel. Off.
heard me say that we
got all three & ought to
get 300% eff. and made
a report that that state-
ment would make a good
story. We are all happy as
we have flown more missions
than any other squadron
in the European theatre,
& we have destroyed 10
bridges, a dam, & dump in

the last ten missions.

July   , 11th Mission

HEADQUARTERS

TWELFTH  AIR FORCE

The Air Medal

is awarded

Edward R. Noland, Jr., First Lieutenant, Air Corps

310th Bombardment Group (M)

by direction of the President, under the provisions of Army Regulation 600-45 as amended, and pursuant to authority vested in me by the Commanding General, Mediterranean Theater of Operations.

Citation

For meritorious achievement while participating
in aerial flight as bombardier of a B-25 type aircraft
during an attack upon a highway and a railroad bridge
at Rubiera, Italy on 6 July 1944. Lieutenant Noland's
proficiency in combat reflects great credit upon himself and the Military Service of the United States.

John K. Cannon
JOHN K. CANNON
Major General, USA
Commanding

G. O. No. 189, 9 October 1944

14 April 1945 Letter about Distinguished Flying Cross and Air Medal and Silver Oak Cluster

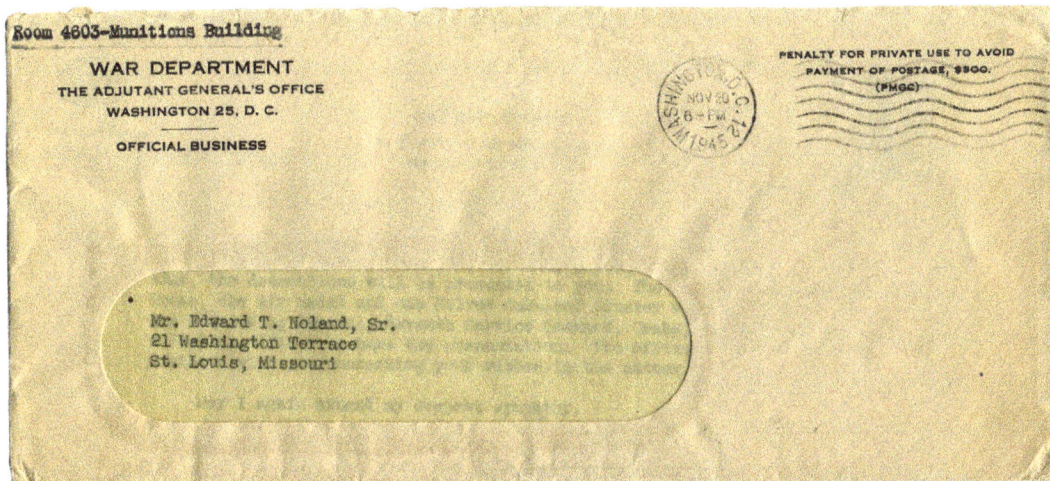

Room 4603-Munitions Building

WAR DEPARTMENT
THE ADJUTANT GENERAL'S OFFICE
WASHINGTON 25, D. C.

OFFICIAL BUSINESS

PENALTY FOR PRIVATE USE TO AVOID
PAYMENT OF POSTAGE, $300.
(PMGC)

Mr. Edward T. Noland, Sr.
21 Washington Terrace
St. Louis, Missouri

SAVE

WAR DEPARTMENT

THE ADJUTANT GENERAL'S OFFICE

IN REPLY REFER TO:

AGPD-R 201 Noland, Edward T., Jr.   WASHINGTON 25, D.C.
01 032 468

FOR VICTORY
BUY
UNITED
STATES
WAR
BONDS
AND
STAMPS

19 April 1945

Mr. Edward T. Noland, Sr.
21 Washington Terrace
St. Louis, Missouri

Dear Mr. Noland:

I have the honor to inform you that, by direction of the President,
the Distinguished Flying Cross, the Air Medal and one Silver Oak-leaf
Cluster, representing five additional awards of the Air Medal, have been
awarded to your son, First Lieutenant Edward T. Noland, Jr., Air Corps.
The citations are as follows:

DISTINGUISHED FLYING CROSS

"For extraordinary achievement while participating in
aerial flight as bombardier of a B-25 type aircraft. On
17 September 1944, Lieutenant Noland flew in an attack upon
an enemy troop and gun concentration near *****, Italy. Upon
the commencement of the bomb run, shell fragments from intense
anti-aircraft fire wounded Lieutenant Noland and hurled him
from position. Quickly recovering himself, Lieutenant Noland,
displaying utmost determination and professional skill, returned
to his bomb sight and released his bombs with precision accuracy
upon this vital objective. On more than fifty-five combat
missions, his outstanding proficiency and steadfast devotion to
duty have reflected great credit upon himself and the Armed Forces
of the United States."

AIR MEDAL AND ONE SILVER OAK-LEAF CLUSTER

"For meritorious achievement while participating as bombardier
in attacks upon ****, Italy on 6 July 1944, ****, Italy on 10 July
1944, ****, Italy on 11 July 1944, ****, Italy on 15 July 1944,
****, Italy 27 July 1944, and ****, Italy on 1 August 1944. In
contributing to these outstanding achievements in precision bombing, the personal courage, professional skill and devotion to duty
displayed by Lieutenant Noland reflect highest credit upon the
Military Service of the United States."

Mr. Edward T. Noland, Sr.
AGPD-R 201 Noland, Edward T., Jr.
01 032 468

    Since these awards cannot be formally presented to your son at this
time, the decorations will be presented to you. The Distinguished Flying
Cross, the Air Medal and one Silver Oak-leaf Cluster will be forwarded to
the Commanding General, Seventh Service Command, Omaha, Nebraska, who will
select an officer to make the presentation. The officer selected will com-
municate with you concerning your wishes in the matter.

    May I again extend my deepest sympathy.

                      Sincerely yours,

                      J. A. ULIO
                      Major General
                      The Adjutant General

2

— APPENDIX K —

11 November 1944 Letter from Tee to his sister Florence

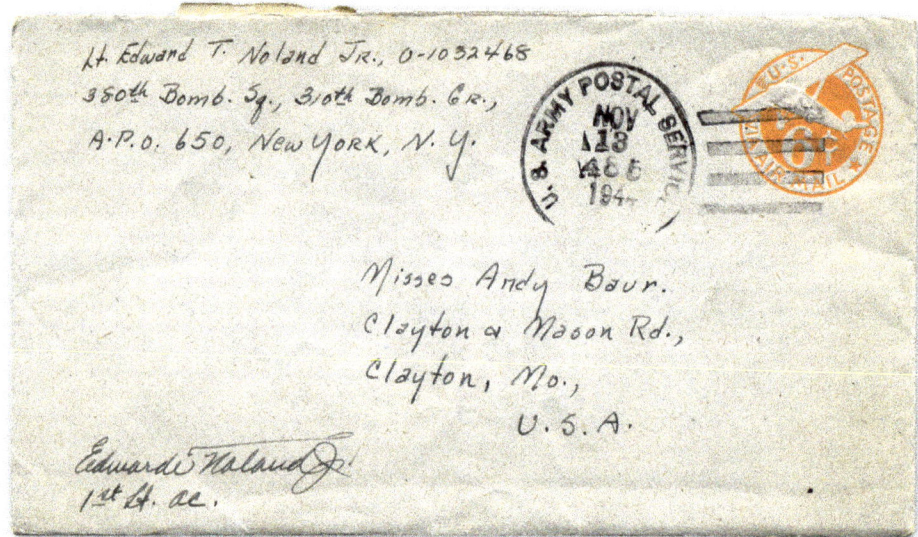

November 11th, 1944.
Corsica.

My Dear Florence.

This is just a note to get you to do me a favor. I will wire or cable some money to you around the end of this month, and it should get there around the 15th of December. I would like for you to buy something for Pat & mail it to her, and buy something for Mam & Pap. There should be enough for something for Jane & Ed too, and please take whatever is left and buy what you want from me.

Don't be a nut about this now.
I am asking you to do it, and by
the time this reaches you the money
will be cabled so there isn't much
you can do about it. Just keep it
under your hat. Thanks.

Here's something else just
between the two of us. I think
the end of my tour over here
is in sight though still far
away. Don't go guessing any time
because you would be wrong. I
would never tell you when I
might be home because anything
can happen, & you remember the
marry on the Stanards. Just keep

it under your shirt, and drop me
a line. In the meantime don't
spit in the wind & tell Andy
hello for me. See you later. Be
good.

all my Love,
Lee.

114

— APPENDIX L —

19 November 1945 Letter of Presumptive Date of Death

WAR DEPARTMENT

THE ADJUTANT GENERAL'S OFFICE

WASHINGTON 25, D. C.

IN REPLY REFER TO:

AGPC-S 201 Noland, Edward T., Jr.
(19 Nov 45) 01032468

19 November 1945

Mrs. Florence Miller Noland
Clayton and Mason Road
Clayton 5, Missouri

Dear Mrs. Noland:

Since your son, First Lieutenant Edward T. Noland, Jr., 01032468, Air Corps, was reported missing in action 18 November 1944, the War Department has entertained the hope that he survived and that information would be revealed dispelling the uncertainty surrounding his absence. However, as in many cases, the conditions of warfare deny us such information. The record concerning your son shows that he was the bombardier aboard a B-25 (Mitchell) aircraft which departed its base in Italy, 18 November 1944, on a combat mission to Casarsa, Italy. Casarsa is located on the Taliamento River in northeastern Italy, approximately forty-five miles north of Venice. At about 1:00 p.m., while over the target, just after bombs had been released, the plane received a direct hit which set the right engine on fire and disabled the ship. Other hits caused the ship to explode and as it went down on fire, it broke in two pieces and landed in the river at Casarsa where it burned. Your son was not one of those who parachuted to safety.

Full consideration has recently been given to all available information bearing on the absence of your son, including all records, reports and circumstances. These have been carefully reviewed and considered. In view of the fact that twelve months have now expired without the receipt of evidence to support a continued presumption of survival, the War Department must terminate such absence by a presumptive finding of death. Accordingly, an official finding of death has been recorded under the provisions of Public Law 490, 77th Congress, approved March 7, 1942, as amended.

The finding does not establish an actual or probable date of death; however, as required by law, it includes a presumptive date of death for the termination of pay and allowances, settlement of accounts and payment of death gratuities. In the case of your son, this date has been set as 19 November 1945, the day following the expiration of twelve months absence.

I regret the necessity for this message but trust that the ending of a long period of uncertainty may give at least some small measure of consolation. I hope you may find sustaining comfort in the thought that the uncertainty with which war has surrounded the absence of your son has enhanced the honor of his service to his country and of his sacrifice.

Sincerely yours,

EDWARD F. WITSELL
Major General
Acting The Adjutant General of the Army

1 Incl.

— APPENDIX M —

Letter & Certificate for Purple Heart

WAR DEPARTMENT
THE ADJUTANT GENERAL'S OFFICE
WASHINGTON 25, D. C.

THE PURPLE HEART AWARDED POSTHUMOUSLY

The Purple Heart was originally established by General George Washington at Newburgh, 7 August 1782, during the War of the Revolution. The decoration was revived by the War Department on 22 February 1932, the two-hundredth anniversary of General Washington's birth, thus paying respect to his memory and recognizing his military achievements. It is awarded to persons who, while serving in any capacity with the Army of the United States, are wounded in action against an enemy of the United States, or who since 6 December 1941 are killed in action, or who die as a direct result of wounds received in action.

The following is a brief description of the Purple Heart: The decoration consists of a purple enameled heart within a bronze border on which is mounted in relief a profile head of General Washington in military uniform. Above the enameled heart is the shield of Washington's coat of arms between two sprays of leaves in green enamel. On the reverse, below the shield and leaves without enamel, is a raised bronze heart with the inscription "For Military Merit," under which is engraved the name of the recipient. The medal is suspended by a rectangular-shaped metal loop with corners rounded from a silk moire ribbon of purple center with white edges.

In posthumous awards of the Purple Heart the Commanding General, Philadelphia Quartermaster Depot, is directed to engrave and ship the decoration direct to the proper next of kin. Usually fifteen days time is required after receipt of notice of award, for the engraving, packaging, and shipping of the decoration.

Recipients of posthumous awards of the Purple Heart may display the decoration in any manner desired, except that decoration is not authorized to be worn by them.

EDWARD F. WITSELL
Major General
Acting The Adjutant General

31 January 1945.

25-23390-75M

President Truman Posthumous Honor with accompanying card.

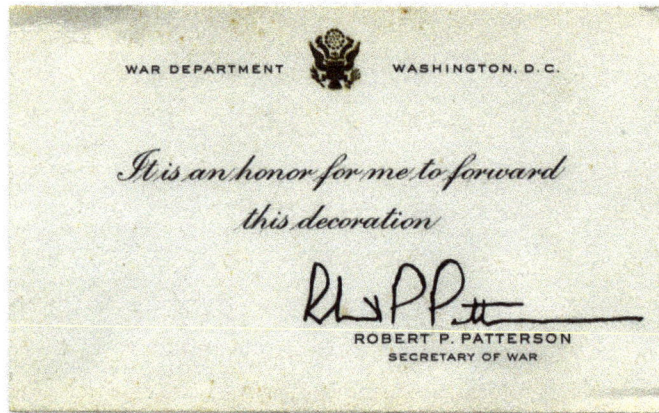

WAR DEPARTMENT · WASHINGTON, D.C.

It is an honor for me to forward
this decoration

ROBERT P. PATTERSON
SECRETARY OF WAR

IN GRATEFUL MEMORY OF

First Lieutenant Edward T. Noland, Jr.

WHO DIED IN THE SERVICE OF HIS COUNTRY

in the Mediterranean Area.

HE STANDS IN THE UNBROKEN LINE OF PATRIOTS WHO HAVE DARED TO DIE

THAT FREEDOM MIGHT LIVE, AND GROW, AND INCREASE ITS BLESSINGS.

FREEDOM LIVES, AND THROUGH IT, HE LIVES—

IN A WAY THAT HUMBLES THE UNDERTAKINGS OF MOST MEN

Harry Truman

PRESIDENT OF THE UNITED STATES OF AMERICA

www.ingramcontent.com/pod-product-compliance
Lightning Source LLC
Chambersburg PA
CBHW061226150426
42812CB00054BA/2531